CITYSPOTS
TALLIN

**Researched and updated by
Scott Diel & Riina Sepp**

Researched and updated by Scott Diel & Riina Sepp

Published by Thomas Cook Publishing
A division of Thomas Cook Tour Operations Limited
Company registration No: 1450464 England
The Thomas Cook Business Park, 9 Coningsby Road
Peterborough PE3 8SB, United Kingdom
Email: books@thomascook.com, Tel: +44 (0)1733 416477
www.thomascookpublishing.com

Produced by The Content Works Ltd
Aston Court, Kingsmead Business Park, Frederick Place
High Wycombe, Bucks HP11 1LA
www.thecontentworks.com

Series design based on an original concept by Studio 183 Limited

ISBN: 978-1-84157-876-7

First edition © 2006 Thomas Cook Publishing
This second edition © 2008 Thomas Cook Publishing
Text © Thomas Cook Publishing
Maps © Thomas Cook Publishing/PCGraphics (UK) Limited
Transport map © Communicarta Limited

Series Editor: Kelly Anne Pipes
Production/DTP: Steven Collins

Printed and bound in Spain by GraphyCems

Cover photography (Tallinn's Old Town church steeples) © Dennis Cox/Alamy

CONTENTS

SYMBOLS KEY

The following symbols are used throughout this book:

ⓐ address ⓣ telephone ⓦ website address ⓛ opening times
ⓝ public transport connections ⓘ important

The following symbols are used on the maps:

ⓘ	information office	▨	points of interest
✈	airport	○	city
✚	hospital	○	large town
◉	police station	○	small town
▣	bus station	═	motorway
▤	railway station	—	main road
✝	cathedral		minor road
❶	numbers denote featured cafés & restaurants	—	railway

Hotels and restaurants are graded by approximate price as follows:
£ budget price ££ mid-range price £££ expensive

Abbreviations used in addresses:

mtn.	maantee (road)
pst.	puiestee (avenue)
tn.	tänav (street)

▶ *Church spires, domes and towers add to Tallinn's enchanting skyline*

INTRODUCING
Tallinn

Introduction

The main reason why the capital of Estonia is such a compelling city to visit right now is that it's at a key point in its evolution. In the last 20 years, the country has experienced a traumatic (if much-welcomed) rupture from Soviet-style communism and has embraced the values of Western-style democratic capitalism. A new country is being born, and the place in which you can most clearly witness the effects of its spectacular evolution is, of course, Tallinn.

But that's just the main reason; there are many others, and not the least of these is the city's proportions, which you might describe as small but intriguingly formed. More petite than, say, Riga and Vilnius, Tallinn can largely be covered on foot. A lot is packed into the city, and most of the major points of interest are within 2 km (just over a mile) of the centre of town. Add to this clean air, clean streets, little traffic congestion and warm and friendly residents; add to that the architectural and cultural heritage created by a thousand years of eventful history and you can see exactly why tourists are waking up to the good news that is Tallinn. However, the city recognises that as it's been forced to hide its attractions under a bushel for so long, it cannot allow cost to prohibit potential visitors from becoming actual ones. Thus it is a comparatively inexpensive destination in which to have a thoroughly good time.

Whatever your area of interest – stunning medieval architecture, fabulously uninhibited nightlife, beautifully unspoilt areas of greenery or the chance to see the remnants of Soviet culture while you still can – Tallinn offers the lot. The city will always be fascinating, but why not treat yourself to a visit now, at this particularly vivid moment in its history?

● *It's not just church roofs that look attractive in the Old Town*

When to go

Tallinn's climate is not one of extremes, and most of the year the weather is amenable. If you don't like the cold, February is the month to avoid; if you don't like it hot you can visit Tallinn at any time of year. October to February can be rather dark months, which limits time for sightseeing, although the darkened, snow-filled city, with warm fireplaces in medieval settings, offers a charm of its own that attracts more and more people every winter.

SEASONS & CLIMATE

Tallinn's climate is controlled by incoming streams of warm water from the Atlantic Ocean, moderated by the Baltic Sea. This gives the city a moderate, maritime climate, with summers not too hot, and winters not too cold. The humidity in summer can be high, up to 80 per cent. Thus, Tallinn tends to be rather cloudy and damp, with an average of about 500 mm (19.5 in) of precipitation a year.

Spring starts in mid-April, and comes in quickly, with an explosion of green in the fields, and multicoloured flowers just about everywhere. July and August, although the warmest months, are also the wettest, with frequent showers. Mid-summer temperatures average 16°C (60°F) and can reach more than 30°C (86°F). Autumn is long and warm.

Winter gets serious in November, and lasts until April, with snow usually on the ground from late December until late March. Winter temperatures average -5°C (23°F) and rarely go over 4°C (39°F). April and October tend to be unpredictable, with both cold, wintry days

⊙ *There's more than a chance of snow early in the year*

and warm, spring-like days. May, June and September are the most comfortable months in which to visit.

But visiting Tallinn at any time of year is rewarding, the run-up to Christmas being especially pleasant.

ANNUAL EVENTS

The summer solstice is the holiday that Estonians anticipate most keenly. The entire country takes time off to revel in the long day of light. Summer days in general are enthusiastically celebrated, with all kinds of music and dance festivals that embrace national and international cultures. It's the time for medieval markets, beer fests and, happily, nights of barely restrained hedonism.

Late autumn and winter don't mean a slowdown in activity for the city: film festivals, concerts and dances simply move indoors.

In December the Tallinn Christmas Market returns to Raekoja Plats (Town Hall Square). A gigantic Christmas tree is the centrepiece of the fair, surrounded by huts selling everything from handicrafts to food. Live performers entertain, and, of course, there's that visit from Santa.

January
Open Music Festival A month-long festival of concerts held in the historical venues of Old Town Tallinn. ☎ 614 7700

April
Estonian Music Days This festival, held in venues around town, is devoted to new music based on classical Estonian works. ☎ 645 4068, 646 6536 🌐 www.helilooja.ee

St George's Day Fair Handicrafts and farm goods are sold on the streets of the Old Town, plus brooms and brushes to get you ready for Walpurgis Night at the end of the month, when witches are said to take to the skies. ☎ 660 4772

Jazzkaar One of Tallinn's best-attended events, this international jazz festival, which takes place in venues all across the city, mixes traditional and cutting-edge music. Organising body the Jazzkaar Friends Society holds other jazz events throughout the year. ☎ 611 4405 ⓦ www.jazzkaar.ee

June

Celebration of St John's Day Bonfires, dancing, music, games and legends are all part of the mid-summer festival celebrating the longest day of the year. ⓐ Estonian Open-air Museum (see page 94) ☎ 654 9100

Old Town Days Every year for four days in the summer, Town Hall Square (see page 76) is turned into a medieval market overflowing

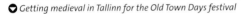
● *Getting medieval in Tallinn for the Old Town Days festival*

with goods, handicrafts and art. Scattered within the confines of the Old Town you'll find people playing the parts of tradesmen, nobles, jesters and musicians. Ⓦ www.vanalinnapaevad.ee

July

Medieval Market In the Old Town, traditional trade folk bring their skills to life while others – almost certainly the same ones who honoured last month's Old Town Days with their presence – dress up in period clothing. ❶ 660 4772 Ⓦ www.folkart.ee

Õllesummer The biggest beer fest in the Baltic comes to Tallinn for five days every summer. Drink deep while listening to rock, reggae, blues, jazz and Estonian music. ❸ Lualuväljak (Song Festival Grounds, see page 97) Ⓦ www.ollesummer.ee

August

August Dance Festival A lively international festival of dancing, highlighting emerging new artists. Events are held mainly at the Kanuti Gildi Saal venue in the Old Town. ❸ Pikk 20 ❶ 646 4704 Ⓦ www.saal.ee

October

International New Music Festival A festival of contemporary music, with around a hundred new works. Held every two years (the next is in 2009) at venues all over the city.

November

Pimedate Ööde Filmifestival (Tallinn Black Nights Film Festival) This combines showings of both professionally produced, feature-length films and the works of students. ❶ 631 4640 Ⓦ www.poff.ee

December

Christmas Jazz Music to cheer the darkest nights kicks off in late
November and continues in various venues throughout December.
For tickets and schedule, see Ⓦ www.jazzkaar.ee

Christmas Market Town Hall Square in the Old Town comes
alive with the sights and sounds of Christmas every day
until 26 December. A huge Christmas tree is the showpiece,
surrounded by huts selling crafts, food, ornaments and toys.
ⓐ Ober-Haus Schlössle ⓣ 679 8585

> **PUBLIC HOLIDAYS**
> **New Year's Day** 1 January
> **Independence Day** 24 February
> **Good Friday** 21 March 2008; 10 April 2009
> **Easter Sunday** 23 March 2008; 12 April 2009
> **Spring Day** 1 May
> **Whit Sunday** 11 May 2008; 31 May 2009
> **Victory Day** 23 June
> **St John's Day** 24 June
> **Day of Restoration of Independence** 20 August
> **Christmas Eve** 24 December
> **Christmas Day** 25 December
> **Second Day of Christmas** 26 December

E-stonia: totally wired

Estonia's ardent embrace of the internet – it's by far the most
e-savvy country in Europe – has caused a societal revolution
which has, in its own way, been every bit as consequential as
the political upheaval that culminated in the country's
independence in 1991.

In fact, internet communication was key to the success of the
late-1980s' revolutionary movement (see page 21): student activists,
who were hip to the then-new technology, used email to organise
protests and meetings, setting up internet points in the countryside
around Tallinn to frustrate government snooping. This is why even
the most remote rural outposts are fully connected today. As soon
as the authorities realised what was going on, they established their
own net-surveillance infrastructure, which was subsequently used
as the foundation for Estonia's post-independence technological
big bang; and what a big big bang it's been.

Today, three-quarters of the population has a mobile phone, and almost a half regularly uses the internet, an astonishing progression when you consider that, 15 years ago, hot water was regarded as a luxury in a lot of places outside Tallinn. By 2010, schools will have one computer for every child – having such a well-educated generation waiting in the wings can only be a good thing for the country's future.

Wireless technology has entered daily life. Estonia's health service monitors people with conditions such as hypertension and diabetes via tiny devices that are inserted into the body and transmit data to healthcare teams. Ironically, the formerly secretive and repressive processes of government have become remarkably open, thanks to e-governance: papers and documents are freely available on the web, and the country has pioneered on-line voting. The 2005 and 2007 elections were carried out using this medium, and both were corruption-free and ran smoothly.

⬇ *Estonia is confident and progressive with most information technology*

History

Due to its strategic location between Eastern and Western Europe, Tallinn has a long and varied history: the vast periods of occupation that Estonia has endured makes its current independence all the more important.

The area around Tallinn was first settled 3,500 years ago by Finno-Ugric migrants. The settlement slowly grew, and by the 10th century it was an important trading city for Scandinavian and Russian merchants. By the middle of the 12th, Tallinn was appearing on world maps.

Next, German 'Knights of the Sword' arrived, bringing with them Christianity and Western European culture. Then, in 1219, Tallinn was conquered by the Danes. The city acquired its current name – from *Taani linn* ('Danish city') – during this period, which also saw the development of *Toompea* ('Dome hill') and its cathedral, and the imposition of the street network that still exists today. In 1285, Tallinn joined the Hanseatic League.

In 1346, Denmark sold Northern Estonia, including Tallinn, to Germany. For the next 200 years (a period known as the 'Golden Age'), Tallinn flourished, and grew into one of the biggest and most powerful towns in Northern Europe, fortified with 66 defensive towers.

The Reformation of 1524 replaced the cultural influence of the Catholic Church with that of the Lutheran, which began school education for the citizens. The Livonian War, a three-party affair between Russia, Poland and Sweden, with Estonia caught in the middle, ended the Golden Age and, in 1561, the Swedes captured Tallinn, although it was another 65 years before all of Estonia fell under Swedish rule. This era was referred to as 'The Good Old Swedish Times', surely ironically, as Tallinn spent it languishing economically. Falling into Russian hands in the Northern War in 1710 was not such a disaster as one might think: the Tsars allowed Tallinn a fair amount of autonomy, and started building it into an important Russian port, as well as developing it as an industrial city.

After World War I and the Russian Revolution, Estonia declared itself independent on 24 February 1918, but it took two years of fighting against both Germany and Russia before the country's independence was recognised by the Tartu Peace Treaty on 2 February 1920. This brief blossom of independence ended with World War II, when first Russia, then Germany, and then Russia once more occupied Estonia.

With the fall of Soviet Russia (signalled by the 'Singing Revolution', see page 21), Estonia once again declared independence on 20 August 1991. The country joined NATO in March of 2004 and then the European Union in May of the same year. Since then, Estonia has taken an active – sometimes vigorous – part in EU affairs. The definitive accolade – admission to the euro – is expected in 2010. Tallinn itself is managing its rapid development into a modern city with dash and brio.

🔻 *Tallinn's citizens are now free to celebrate their culture*

Lifestyle

What a difference a decade makes: only ten or so years ago you would find people having to queue for such necessities as toothpaste and tomatoes. Now there are major department stores and shopping centres, expensive cars parked on cobble-stoned streets and a population that's more than happy to welcome a flood of visitors.

Estonians may seem a somewhat shy people until they get to know you. In terms of how you should approach them initially, a good rule is to be friendly, but never over-familiar. They are, really, fun-loving and outgoing. You'll observe their exuberance in the café and bar scene that is a huge part of everyday Estonian life; expect thought-provoking dialogues from well-educated locals in the cafés during the day and lively party scenes in the clubs and pubs at night. Tallinn seems to hold more (and longer) festivals than any other country in the Baltics.

Estonians are remarkably high-tech. They use the internet more than any other country in the world – thus the soubriquet 'E-stonia'

THE GOOD GUEST'S GUIDE
Estonians can be a little shy, so don't take it personally if you attend a party and no-one offers their hand. Younger Estonians have more quickly adopted this Western custom, but older ones have not. If you're invited into someone's home, count yourself lucky, as this has great meaning in a culture where most people simply keep to themselves. When entering someone's home, always remove your shoes (since streets in Tallinn used to be dirty, it is considered a courtesy to remove footwear). It is generally the custom for guests to bring flowers.

(see page 14). Technology aside, if you ask an Estonian his or her idea of a good time, the reply might well be 'a walk in the woods' or 'a day spent fishing'. For all their urban lifestyle and Wi-Fi technology, Estonians are naturalists at heart.

⬤ *Alfresco cafés have sprung up all around the city*

Culture

Tallinn cannot rival metropolises like London or New York in size or international standing, but it doesn't let that stand in its way. Live theatre, opera, symphony, folk music, choirs, art, newspapers, magazines and, of course, the dialogues in the coffee houses are

● *The Song Festival Grounds celebrate a key facet of Estonian life*

THE SINGING REVOLUTION

Song festivals have played a massive role in Baltic life since the 19th century, when the rediscovery of folk songs started to rejuvenate the indigenous cultures that had been weakened by centuries of foreign domination. During the Soviet period, singing festivals were the only expression of national solidarity that were tolerated.

In 1988, the labour unions and the Estonian Heritage Society organised a massive Song Festival at the Lauluväljak (Song Festival Grounds) in Tallinn (see page 97). The festival became the focus of mass demonstrations against the Soviet regime. This movement became known as the 'Singing Revolution', and the term was used to describe the independence movement in all three Baltic States – Estonia, Latvia and Lithuania.

Perhaps the greatest demonstration of inter-Baltic solidarity occurred on 23 August 1989, when two million people joined hands to form a human chain stretching from Tallinn to Vilnius. Song festivals are still held, and still pack a potent emotional punch, now that independence is well assured.

all parts of Estonia's complex, lively, and ever-evolving cultural scene. Since Estonia regained its independence with the fall of the Soviet Union, cultural life has begun a rapid evolution, embracing all kinds of new media and virtual art. Yet it continues to hold dear its traditions. Every four years the Quadrennial Song and Dance Festival takes place in Tallinn, beginning with a festive parade of performers to the Song Festival Grounds located in the suburb of Pirita (see page 96).

Music is a major part of Estonian life, and both the National Symphony Orchestra and National Opera have earned solid reputations worldwide. Aside from the traditional concert hall venues of the Great and Small Guilds, the Old Town has a plethora of atmospheric sites for music, including medieval churches.

Music is more than just a part of the Estonian culture, however: it is the frame that holds the tapestry of culture in this country. The tradition of folk music is centuries old, and Estonia boasts one of the largest collections of folk songs in the world, with written records of some 133,000 songs. It is no wonder that the country's break from the Soviets came with the 'Singing Revolution'.

Live theatre is another favourite pastime of Tallinn residents. From the traditional **Estonian Drama Theatre** (❸ Parnu mnt. 5 ❶ 683 1413 ❿ www.draamateater.ee) to the cutting-edge presentations of the **Salong-Theatre** (❿ www.slong-teater.ee) and **Theatre NO99** (❸ Sakala 3 ❶ 668 8781), Estonians appear to embrace drama in all its forms. Youngsters are introduced to live theatre at the Estonian Puppet Theatre (see page 148). A truly avant-garde experience is the **Von Krahl Theatre** (❿ www.vonkrahl.ee), which performs in a cabaret-like hall.

Estonians are also avid readers, and they like to keep themselves well informed. The Tallinn Central Library, which opened in 1907 and has more than 20 branches (for a city of less than 500,000 people), is one of the oldest in Estonia.

❿ *The colourful clock face of the Church of the Holy Ghost*

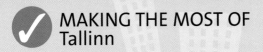

Shopping

If you last visited Tallinn when the Soviets were in charge, you're in for a surprise: the shopping scene has changed exponentially, and the city certainly doesn't lack for any number of places to spend your money these days. The Old Town (see page 68) is filled with dozens of souvenir, antiques, clothing and speciality shops.

The most popular souvenir items are knitted goods like sweaters and mittens, patchwork quilts, trinkets bearing the city name, and spirits. For a truly authentic Estonian souvenir, purchase a Kihnu Island sweater (see below). The main shopping streets in the Old Town are Viru, Müürivahe, Suur-Karja, plus Kullassepa near Town Hall Square.

You'll also find craftsmen plying their wares along Müürivahe in the Old Town. Their prices are sometimes cheaper, and the

KIHNU ISLAND SWEATERS
Kihnu is an island off Estonia's western coast which has a long history of producing beautiful knitwear. These beautiful, warm sweaters are unique in design (often blue-and-white or black-and-white) with decorative collars, and make ideal souvenirs or presents. The best place to buy one is from the charming old women who man the stands on Müürivahe Street near the Viru Gates. Bargaining is usually fruitless, unless you're planning on purchasing larger quantities.

▶ *Medieval fairs are a marketplace for traditional crafts and foodstuffs*

USEFUL SHOPPING PHRASES

What time do the shops open/close?
Mis kell kauplused avatakse/suletakse?
Mis kell kah-up-lused ahvah-tahk-se/su-letahk-se?

How much is this?
Kui palju see maksab?
Kuy pal-yu se-eh mak-sab?

Can I try this on?
Kas ma tohin seda proovida?
Kas mah toh-hin seh-da pro-o-vi-da?

My size is ...
Minu number on . . .
Mi-nuh nub-ber on . . .

I'll take this one, thank you
Aitäh, ma võtan selle
Ay-tahh, mah vo-tan sel-leh

Can you show me the one in the window/this one?
Näidake mulle palun seda vaateaknalt/seda?
Nay-da-keh mul-leh pah-loon seh-da vah-ah-te-ahk-nalt/seh-da?

This is too large/too small/too expensive
See on liiga suur/liiga väike/liiga kallis
Se-eh on lee-ga su-ur/lee-ga vay-keh/lee-ga kal-lis

salespeople (generally older women) even more charming than most you'll meet in the shops.

At the other end of the retail scale, you'll find plucky, small-scale entrepreneurs hawking postcards outside nearly every tourist attraction. A flea market near the Old Town can turn up such lovely finds as a pure linen poncho or leather goods, and if you feel that a Russian-made fur hat would set you off, this is a good place to look.

Stockmann and Kaubamaja (see page 88), the two largest department stores in town, sell everything you could desire, from clothing and cosmetics to electronics. These locations are your best bet for any item you left at home.

Don't overlook the shopping centres, which can be glitzy and airy. The newest is Viru Keskus (see page 88), which contains the largest bookshop in the Baltics, an art gallery and the usual stores. The **Kristine Centre** (Ⓐ Endla 45 Ⓦ www.kristiinekeskus), meanwhile, has clothing, grocery and speciality stores all in one place. For upmarket chic in the Old Town, try the smaller **Demini Centre** (Ⓐ Viru 1), which is a good place to purchase handicrafts to take home.

Probably the tourists' most popular purchase is amber, and you'll find countless places to buy this Baltic treasure. But telling real from fake requires deft application of a flame – plastic melts, amber doesn't – and it's a person of rare personal charm who can get away with starting a fire in a foreign shop.

Eating & drinking

Estonian cuisine is rich in meat, potatoes and dairy products, with pork, cheese and sour cream involved in some manner with almost every dish. Rye bread, salted herring and beer are also traditional foods.

A traditional Estonian starter is *sült*, a mixture of pork pieces set in jelly. It is an acquired taste. Most restaurants feature salted herring, smoked eel and sliced sausage, all served with delicious dark rye bread, as a starter.

Soup can be either a starter or a snack for lunch. The most common soup is *seljanka*, a Russian broth of meat, pickled vegetables and fish. Other light meals include *pelmeenid* (akin to Italian ravioli), *pirukad* (dough stuffed with bacon and cabbage) and pancakes with cheese, meat or mushrooms. Salads are becoming more common. You may want to try a traditional Estonian salad of peas and pickles served in sour cream. Plates of greens, often laced with tuna, are also a local favourite.

The standard Estonian main course is pork with potatoes and *sauerkraut*. The pork comes either as roast, or as a chop in batter. It usually has a good rind of fat which, when properly cooked, is delicious. Other meat courses, based on beef, chicken and blood

PRICE CATEGORIES

The restaurant price guides used in this book indicate the approximate cost of a three-course meal for one person, excluding drinks.

£ up to 20kr. ££ 20–30kr. £££ over 30kr.

🔺 *Tallinn's cafés and bars range from traditional to downright trendy*

sausage, are common, as are pan-fried freshwater fish such as trout, perch and pike.

Vegetarians shouldn't despair, although their options may be somewhat limited. A few exclusively vegetarian restaurants have opened, but, sadly, all of them failed. Tallinn's restaurants, though, are becoming more used to vegetarian customers and generally have something on the menu. The best bet is to head to other ethnic eateries. As Tallinn becomes more cosmopolitan, a much wider variety of ethnic foods from around the world is becoming available, with French, Italian, Greek, Indian, Japanese and Chinese restaurants, to name a few, already well established.

Estonians love their sweets. The most common dessert is *mannapuder* (semolina pudding), often served with fruits and berries. Pancakes filled with jam are another local favourite. Cakes, flans, tarts and cheesecake are widely available.

On the liquid side, the Estonians prefer coffee or soft drinks in the daytime, and beer in the evening. (They customarily take their coffee black: if you want cream or sugar, you will have to ask for it.) Espresso and cappuccino are available, but filter coffee is most common in restaurants where large numbers of tourists are served. Locals often accompany their coffee with a sticky bun or piece of cake.

There is an increasing number of bars and pubs in Tallinn, most in the English and American style. The beer normally comes as a regular lager, and the locals consume a lot of it. Stronger beers and ales are also available. Beer is normally sold by the half-litre (that's nearly a pint), and ordering lesser amounts is frowned upon. A traditional Estonian spirit is *Vana Tallinn*. A rather syrupy and medicinal liqueur, it is easier to drink watered down with fruit juice or coffee; some find it quite tasty mixed with champagne. Thanks to the Russian influence, good vodka is also readily available, and at good prices.

Restoran, meaning restaurant, indicates a more upmarket establishment, complete with menus and table service. There are many of these in Tallinn, including in most major hotels. For something more informal, try a café, where you order and pay at the counter. Many pubs and bars also offer a full menu.

With Tallinn's abundance of green spaces and parks, especially adjacent to the Old Town, you should try a picnic in the park one sunny afternoon.

USEFUL DINING PHRASES

I would like a table for ... people
Ma soovin lauda ... inimesele
Mah so-ov-in lau-da ...ih-ni-meh-seh-leh

Waiter/waitress!	**May I have the bill, please?**
Kelner! Ettekandja!	Ma palun arve?
Kelner! Ettekandyah!	*Mah pah-loon ar-veh?*

Could I have it well-cooked/medium/rare please?
Palun praadige liha tugevalt/keskmiselt/pooltooreks?
*Pah-loon pra-a-di-ghe ly-hah tuh-ghe-valt/kesk-mi-selt/
poh-ohl-toh-oh-reks?*

I am a vegetarian.	**Where is the toilet**
Does this contain meat?	**(restroom) please?**
Ma olen taimetoitlane.	Palun, kus asub WC?
Kas see sisaldab liha?	*Pah-loon, kus a-sup*
Mah olen tayme-toytlane.	*veh-tseh?*
Kahs se-eh see-sahl-dahb liha?	

I would like a cup of/two cups of/another coffee/tea
Ma palun ühe tassi/kaks tassi/veel kohvi/teed
Mah pah-loon u-heh tas-si/kaks tas-si/ve-el koh-vi/te-ed

I would like a beer/two beers, please
Palun üks õlu/kaks õlut
Pah-loon uks oh-lyuh/kaks oh-lyuht

Entertainment & nightlife

Don't be surprised that a small city can have such a variety of nightlife and after-hours entertainment available. Tallinn seems capable of accommodating almost every taste, from the ear-splitting rock of a packed nightclub to the quiet sophistication of a cigar and brandy lounge.

Most of the nightlife is in and around Tallinn's Old Town. You won't need to make plans to visit a specific club; simply wander from place to place until you find one that suits your style. Some are just metres apart from each other.

Timing is everything. Friday is the night to party in Tallinn. Thursdays and Saturdays are also quite lively, but the rest of the week can be almost dull by comparison to Friday. During the week the bars are usually open only until midnight and some clubs don't even bother to open on a Sunday, Monday or Tuesday.

Tallinn's cultural life outside the bar is also wide and varied. The National Symphony and National Opera are two stalwarts that can be counted on for quality performances. You'll also discover that the small venues of the Old Town include churches that offer medieval and Early Music performances. Chamber music concerts are frequently held in the House of the Blackheads.

Theatre is not to be overlooked in the city, although most of the performances will be in Estonian. If you can spend an evening enthralled in stage craft, you'll not want to miss the chance of attending a play or two.

A live performance of music will transcend any language barriers, and Tallinn boasts no shortage of concerts and performances. Yes, you'll find lots of classical and operatic music, but Tallinn is heavily into jazz, pop and all kinds of contemporary sounds.

Need your entertainment on a big screen? Tallinn is home to the Dark Nights Film Festival, held in December. During the rest of the year, many multiplex theatres show both mainstream and art films, many in English with Estonian subtitles. The **Kosmos** (ⓐ Pärnu mnt. 45 ⓣ 680 0566 ⓦ www.forumcinemas.ee) features mostly Hollywood fare; try the **Sõprus** (ⓐ Vana-Posti 8 ⓣ 644 1919 ⓦ www.kino.ee) or **Kinomaja** (ⓐ Uus 3 ⓣ 646 4068 ⓦ www.kinomaja.ee) for more avant-garde selections.

🔺 *Tallinn has many live music performances*

Sport & relaxation

SPECTATOR SPORTS

Basketball and football are the two most popular spectator sports in Estonia, with the latter enjoying a definite vogue as the national team gets better and better.

Basketball, hockey and other sports take place in the Saku Suurhall Arena (see page 86).

Football matches are held at A. Le Coq Arena, which is about thirty minutes by foot to the southwest of the city centre. ❸ Asula 4c

Horse racing, especially trotting with sulkies (two-wheeled carts), is popular in Tallinn. Racing takes place at the **Tallinn Hippodrome**. ❸ Paldiski mnt. 50 ❶ 677 1677 🌐 www.hipodroom.ee ❷ Trolleybus: 6, 7; bus: 21

PARTICIPATION SPORTS

In the summer months, Estonians take to the great outdoors, with hiking, canoeing, cycling and bird watching popular activities. Most of this is done well outside Tallinn in places such as Lahemaa National Park (see page 122), **Soomaa National Park** (🌐 www.soomaa.com), or along the many kilometres of Baltic coastline. These areas have

WINTER SPORTS

With the long winters, skiing is popular in Estonia. The best skiing is cross-country, as there are few hills high enough for a good downhill run. Otepää, in southern Estonia, is the leading ski resort. Estonia came second on the medals table of the 2006 Winter Olympics.

🔺 *Gamblers bet on sulky racing on-line, as well as at the Hippodrome*

well-maintained hiking trails and nature paths. Deer, moose and elk are commonly sighted along these trails, as are the occasional bear and wild boar.

Exercise and fitness are big in Estonia. Some major hotels feature exercise facilities and swimming pools. If you want to jog, stick to Pirita and Kadriorg, as other areas of the city are dimly lit, and have many dogs on the loose. Tallinn has several clubs that offer aerobics, weightlifting and yoga, and many have swimming pools and saunas.

Facilities for basketball, billiards, bowling, cycling, horse riding, ice skating, swimming, skating, squash and tennis are also available in the city – the tourist office can provide details (see page 153).

RELAXATION

Most of Estonia takes the month of August off to go to summer houses in the countryside. If you should happen not to get an invitation, there are plenty of spas in and around Tallinn where relaxation is guaranteed (see page 136).

Accommodation

New hotels are springing up like daisies to accommodate the ever-growing tourist demand. As a rule of thumb, the most luxurious establishments are located in the Old Town area, with more economical choices found in the city centre and in the suburbs. Some of the budget hotels are products of the Soviet era and are not likely to have been renovated. Hotels, especially in summer, should be booked months in advance.

HOTELS

Dzingel ££ A large, somewhat remodelled Soviet hotel in Tallinn's Nõmme garden district. It has all the services you'd expect at a Western hotel, though it's a bit worn around the edges. Still, it's a civilised way to have an up-close look at Soviet architecture. ❸ Männiku tee 89 ❶ 610 5201 Ⓦ www.dzingel.ee Ⓝ Bus: 5

Hotel G9 ££ Located on the third floor of a Stalinist-era office building, this is a simple hotel with very basic services (but an excellent kebab restaurant). The price is right and the city-centre location fab. ❸ Gonsiori 9 ❶ 626 7130 or 626 7131 Ⓦ www.hotelg9.ee Ⓝ Bus: 1A, 5, 8, 34A, 38, 51, 60, 63

PRICE CATEGORIES
The ratings below indicate the approximate cost of a room for two people for one night.
£ under 35kr.   ££ 35–60kr.   £££ 60–120kr.   £££+ over 120kr.

Meriton Old Town Hotel ££ A nice hotel on the edge of the
Old Town. The rooms are somewhat small but cheerful in décor.
The lobby contains part of the old city wall and the round outer
edge of the neighbouring 15th-century mill. ⊟ Lai 49 ☎ 614 1300
🖤 www.meritonhotels.com

Pirita Cloister Guesthouse ££ Run by the nuns of the St Bridgettine
Order, this is not recommended for those who want to party;
but for those who want a quiet night's sleep, it's perfect. Located
in the cloister in the Tallinn suburb of Pirita. ⊟ Merivälja tee 18
☎ 605 5000 🖤 www.piritaklooster.ee 🅝 Bus: 1A from the centre

Reval Inn ££ An easily accessible hotel on the edge of the port
and close to the Old Town. The interiors are based on Scandinavian
practicality and minimalism. ⊟ Sadama 1 ☎ 669 0690
🖤 www.revalinn.com 🅝 Bus: 2, 20

Domina City ££–£££ An elegant hotel tucked into the Old Town.
The influence is clearly Italian, with light marble floors and sweeping
staircases. ⊟ Vana-Posti 11/13 ☎ 681 3900 🖤 www.dominahotels.com

Romeo Family Hotel ££–£££ The only family-run hotel in the
Old Town offers a level of personal service that's hard to beat.
The breakfast area, like the rooms, has a nice cosy atmosphere.
⊟ Suur-Karja 18, 4th floor, Apt. 38 ☎ 644 4255

Stroomi ££–£££ A great hotel just yards from the beach and ten
minutes' drive west of the city centre. It rents out bicycles and
roller skates as well. ⊟ Randla 11 ☎ 630 4200 🖤 www.stroomi.ee
🅝 Bus: 40, 48

Uniquestay ££–£££ A well-planned city-centre hotel that has everything you might want, including a computer in each room. The cosy café/restaurant in the basement is worth visiting even if you're not staying in the hotel. ❸ Toompuiestee 23 ❶ 660 0700 ❿ www.uniquestay.com ❿ Bus: 21, 21B, 40

Uniquestay Mihkli ££–£££ The sister hotel of the above has clean, Scandinavian design and flat-screen computers in every room. Excellent value for money. ❸ Endla 23 ❶ 666 4800 ❿ www.uniquestay.com ❿ Trolleybus: 4

⬤ *Reputedly the tallest building in Estonia – the Radisson hotel*

Baltic Hotel Vana Wiru £££ With its spacious rooms with satellite TV, marbled floors and Wi-Fi in the lobby, this Old Town hotel is living proof that traditional can seamlessly blend with techno. ⓐ Viru 11 ⓣ 669 1500 ⓦ www.vanawiru.ee

Old Town Maestro's £££ A six-storey boutique hotel in the heart of the Old Town's night scene that features art deco-influenced interiors and spacious rooms. ⓐ Suur-Karja 10 ⓣ 626 2000 ⓦ www.maestrohotel.ee

Scandic Palace £££ Part of the Hilton International chain, so expect a good room. The location is terrific, right on the edge of the Old Town. ⓐ Vabaduse väljak 3 ⓣ 640 7300 ⓦ www.scandic-hotels.ee Ⓝ Tram: 3, 4

Scandic St Barbara £££ This hotel doesn't boast much in the way of frills but the rooms are comfortable and the location is great, on the edge of the Old Town. If you need to stay connected, there's a computer in the lobby for guest use. ⓐ Roosikrantsi 2a ⓣ 640 7600 Ⓝ Tram: 3, 4

Villa Hortensia £££ A guesthouse in a recently renovated Old Town master's courtyard and a pleasantly unusual find. The hotel shares its location with a gallery and artisans' workshops, which attracts an artistic clientele. As there is no reception at the guesthouse, you need to phone ahead for the keys. ⓐ Vene 6 ⓣ 504 6113

L'Ermitage £££–£££+ Small and traditional, this is a wonderful place to hide away. The rooms have lots of creature comforts such as internet connection and flatscreen TVs. It's also clean, efficient and downright friendly. Centrally located in the Old Town, just west of Toompea Hill. ⓐ Toompuiestee 19 ⓘ 699 6400 ⓦ www.lermitagehotel.ee ⓝ Bus: 21, 21B, 40

Radisson SAS Hotel Tallinn £££–£££+ You shouldn't have any difficulties finding a room in what is said to be the tallest building in the country. It's a business hotel, with health club and sauna, and the location is good for both Old Town and the city centre. The views from the roof-top bar are stunning. Children under 17 stay for free. ⓐ Rävala 3 ⓘ 682 3000 ⓦ www.radissonsas.com ⓝ Trolleybus: 1, 3, 6

Hotel Schlössle £££+ Truly a medieval setting. Heavy wooden beams, massive stone fireplaces and wrought-iron chandeliers are just a few of the touches that give this small hotel its baronial ambience. If the view doesn't sweep you off your feet, the price might. ⓐ Pühavaimu 13/15 ⓘ 699 7700 ⓦ www.schlossle-hotels.com

Hotel St Petersbourg £££+ Dating back to 1850, this is Tallinn's oldest continuously functioning hotel. The interiors are amazing, and the staff are great. The location is hard to beat, too: very close to the epicentre of the Old Town, with everything within easy reach. ⓐ Rataskaevu 7 ⓘ 628 6500 ⓦ www.schlossle-hotels.com

Kolm Õde £££+ An outstanding boutique hotel located inside three of the best-known medieval buildings in Estonia. Known locally as

● *Kolm Õde in the fairytale Three Sisters*

the Three Sisters, the buildings look as though they have stepped straight out of a fairy tale. Inside, the hotel offers comfort in very stylish, individually designed rooms ⓐ Pikk 71/ Tolli 2 ⓣ 630 6300 ⓦ www.threesistershotel.com

◗ Hotels in the medieval streets of the Old Town

Telegraaf £££+ Located in Tallinn's old telegraph station, this 5-star hotel is the only one in the Old Town with underground parking. An Elemis spa, swimming pool and Wi-Fi in every room make this hotel a favourite of those travelling on expense accounts. 🅰 Vene 9 ☎ 640 7300 🆆 www.telegraafhotel.com

HOSTELS

The Estonian Youth Hostel Association is at 🅰 Tatari 39 ☎ 646 1595 🆆 www.balticbookings.com/eyha 🚌 Bus: 3, 16

City Bike Hostel £ Located on a charming street on the edge of the Old Town, City Bike offers excellent room rates, but can also organise bicycle travel and tours to just about anywhere in Estonia. 🅰 Uus 33 ☎ 683 6383 🆆 www.citybike.ee

Eurohostel £ Near Town Hall Square, this is an excellent Old Town choice for backpackers and budget travellers. The interiors are simple and there are both double rooms and dorms that sleep four to six people. 🅰 Nunne 2 ☎☎ 644 7788 🆆 www.eurohostel.ee

Merevaik £ This hostel is known for its friendliness. It's not the easiest to find, but it's worth it when you do for its price. Take trolleybus no. 2 or 3 from the centre to the Linnu tee stop. Follow the swallow signs (landmark Pääsu Hotel) and go around the corner. 🅰 Sõpruse pst. 182 ☎ 655 3767 🆆 www.hostelmerevaik.ee

Tallinn Backpackers £ A hostel that always scores high for camaraderie, a bonus for people travelling alone. Has a free sauna and kitchen computer. 🅰 Lai 10 ☎ 644 0298 🆆 www.tallinnbackpackers.com

THE BEST OF TALLINN

Tallinn is a compact city, so it's easy to visit the key sights.

TOP 10 ATTRACTIONS

- **Toompea Castle** Sitting at the very top of Toompea Hill, Toompea Castle stands as a sentry that for most of Tallinn's history has guarded the city. It is dominated by three defensive towers, the tallest of which, 'Tall Herman', dates from 1371 and proudly flies the Estonian flag (see page 78)

- **St Nicholas's Church** Begun in the 13th century, and rebuilt in the 15th century, this imposing church is now a museum for Tallinn's collection of medieval art (see page 77)

- **Kadriorg** This beautiful park, containing a palace that houses the Museum of Foreign Art, was built by Tsar Peter the Great (see page 92)

- **Raekoda & Raekoja plats (Town Hall & Town Hall Square)** is as old as Tallinn itself. Surrounded by medieval buildings painted in pastel colours, the square is a popular rallying point for Estonian patriotism (see page 76)

- **Alexander Nevsky Cathedral** Built in 1900, this onion-domed Russian Orthodox Church can be seen from most parts of the city (see page 68)

- **Great Sea Gate** At the very northern end of the Old Town, the Great Sea Gate is a 16th-century arch flanked by two towers. The larger of the two towers is called Fat Margaret (see page 74)

- **House of the Blackheads** The Brotherhood of the Blackheads was a merchants' guild founded in 1343, and the house was built to accommodate visiting businessmen. The house is elaborately decorated in Renaissance style, both inside and out (see page 74)

- **Botanical Gardens** Located in Pirita, the gardens feature a large area dedicated to virtually every type of tree and plant found in Estonia, and then some (see page 96)

- **Estonian Open-air Museum** Located on the western outskirts of Tallinn, this is an ethnographic collection of over a hundred 18th- and 19th-century buildings uprooted from around Estonia and brought to this one spot (see page 94)

- **Church of the Holy Ghost** Built in the 1360s, this is the only church in Tallinn whose exterior remains in its original form (see page 70)

◆ *Find a good vantage point for an aerial view of the city*

Suggested itineraries

HALF-DAY: TALLINN IN A HURRY

If your time for sightseeing is limited to only a few hours, you're in luck as many of the city's top attractions are bunched quite close together. There is no logical way to wander the streets, so use Raekoja plats (Town Hall Square, see page 76) as a hub and take side trips out and back.

First, explore Town Hall Square. There are two buildings of interest: the Town Hall to the south, and the Town Council Pharmacy to the north. Behind the Town Hall is the Museum of Photography (see page 80). There are also lots of coffee shops and souvenir stands here. Just a few steps south of the square is the Tourist Office, where you can pick up a map of the city.

The first excursion will be to Toompea. This is the toughest part of the trip, as it features a steep climb. Going west out of the Square, you come to Pikk Street. Continue west until you reach the gate tower once used to keep the local peasants out of Toompea. Go through the gate and climb up along Pikk Jalg Street. At the top you come to Alexander Nevsky Cathedral (see page 68). Walk round the cathedral to find Toompea Castle (see page 78). Then walk north along Toomkooli until you come to Kiriku plats, with the Lutheran Cathedral, **Cathedral of Saint Mary the Virgin** (🚇 Toom-Kooli 6 🕙 644 4140 🌐 www.eelk.ee/tallinna.toom). Take one of the streets on either side of the museum, and you will come to a lookout on the top of the wall that gives a good view of the harbour and the Old Town. Now, retrace your steps to Town Hall Square.

The second trip will take you north. Next to the Town Council Pharmacy is a small alley (Saiakang) that leads to the Church of the Holy Ghost (see page 70). Northwest of the Church is Pikk Street,

and here you will find the **House of the Great Guild** (ⓐ Pikk 17
ⓘ 641 1630 ⓦ www.eam.ee). Continue northeast on Pikk for the
House of the Blackheads (see page 74), Oleviste Kirik (St Olaf's
Church, see page 76), the Three Sisters and, finally, the Great
Sea Gate and the Maritime Museum (see page 73).

Start to retrace your steps, but turn right at the Three Sisters
(Tolli Street), and then left on Lai Street. Here you will see high-gabled
merchants' houses, then turn right on Suur-Kloostri Street to find
the Church of the Transfiguration (see page 70). Turn left on Väike-
Kloostri Street for a good look at the remnants of the city wall, then
left on Nunne Street until you come to the gate tower, and then
head back to Town Hall Square.

The third trip takes you south from Town Hall Square along
Kullassepa Street to St Nicholas's Church (see page 77). West of the
church is Lühike Jalg Street, which heads up to the Adamson-Eric
Museum (see page 78). Come back down and head south and then
east on Rüütli Street, and continue east on Müürivahe Street to see
Museum of Theatre and Music. Return west to Harju Street. You can
now go north on Harju to get back to Town Hall Square, or go south
to Vabaduse väljak.

1 DAY: TIME TO SEE A LITTLE MORE

Once you've visited all the Old Town sights, then you can venture
into the suburbs of Tallinn. The three trips listed below should each
take about three-quarters of a day.

Top of the list would be Kadriorg Park (see page 94), which is
about 1 km (half a mile) due east of the Old Town. On the way, stop
at the Anton Hansen Tammsaare Memorial Museum at Koidula 12a
(see page 88). Once you are in the Kadriorg Park grounds, see the
Eduard Vilde Memorial Museum (ⓐ Roheline Aas 3 ⓘ 601 3181

Ⓦ www.linnamuuseum.ee/vilde), Kadriorg Palace (see page 92), Peter the Great's House and the ornamental garden. Just outside the park are the Song Festival Grounds (see page 97).

A second trip takes you about 2 or 3 km (1.5–2 miles) east of the Old Town and into Pirita. First you will encounter Maarjamäe Palace, which now houses part of the Estonian History Museum (see page 73). In Pirita itself, you will find a huge yachting marina, Pirita Beach and the Botanical Gardens (see page 96). Be sure to visit the observation platform on the television tower for a great view of Tallinn.

A third trip takes you west to the upmarket suburb of Rocca al Mare, about 6 km (4 miles) west of the Old Town. Here you will find Tallinn Zoo (see page 147) and the Estonian Open-air Museum (see page 94).

HERE COME THE STAG WEEKENDERS

With relatively inexpensive flights from London to Tallinn, an increasing number of young British men are flocking to Tallinn for weekend stag parties. Tour companies specialising in this type of entertainment lure them with promises of good, clean and cheap merriment.

These vivacious fun-lovers show up as groups of modern-day ratpackers, flitting from pub to pub like butterflies and generally whooping it up. Favourite spots of these wandering bands of dolce viters include Molly Malones on the square and most any of the larger bars on Viru or Suur-Karja Streets. Long live the stag weekenders, and long may they enliven Friday and Saturday nights.

Serious art fans should not miss **Kumu** (ⓐ Weizenbergi 34/Valge 1 ⓣ 602 6001 ⓦ www.ekm.ee ⓝ Tram: 1, 3; bus: 31, 67, 68), Estonia's national art museum, which opened in 2006. The museum is cut into a limestone cliff and seems to serve as a bridge between historic Tallinn (beneath) and Soviet Tallinn (above).

2–3 DAYS: TIME TO SEE MUCH MORE

If you have several days, you may want to explore the surrounding countryside. Lahemaa National Park (see page 122) is about an hour's drive (70 km/43 miles) east of Tallinn and has a full range of facilities and accommodation. As well as many well-marked hiking and nature trails, there are beach resorts and even a couple of restored palaces.

LONGER: ENJOYING TALLINN TO THE FULL

Once you've explored the city, head out west or south. Although a car is the best way to get around, all places described here have regular bus services from Tallinn.

If you want a few days at a beach resort, then Pärnu, 'Estonia's Summer Capital', is the only place to go (see page 100). The city has a 7 km (4 1/2 mile) beach, which is packed with sunbathers in July and August.

For unspoiled landscape you should travel to the Estonian Islands in the Baltic, namely Vormsi, Hiiumaa, Saaremaa and Muhu. The islands are sparsely populated, accommodation is minimal, and local public transport is non-existent. Plan on taking a car, and, if going in summer, make sure you have reserved accommodation.

For the intellectually inclined, a day or two in Tartu (see page 116) is a must.

Something for nothing

Visit the Old Town and spend an hour or two wandering the steep streets of the medieval core of the city. Marvel at the construction of the buildings that has allowed them not only to last the centuries but also to adapt to new uses such as art galleries and cafés.

City Gallery (☎ Harju 13 ☏ 644 2818 ⏱ 12.00−18.00 Wed−Mon, closed Tues) is noted for its frequently changing contemporary and experimental exhibitions. Best of all, it's free. **Draakoni Gallery (Dragon's Gallery)** (☎ Pikk 18 ☏ 646 4141 ⏱ 10.00−18.00 Mon−Fri, 10.00−17.00 Sat, closed Sun) holds small exhibitions of local and international artists in its beautiful Old Town location which is decorated with dragons carved from stone. In the **National Library of Estonia** (☎ Tõnismägi 2 ⏱ 10.00−20.00 Mon−Fri, 12.00−19.00 Sat, closed Sun (winter); 12.00−19.00 Mon−Fri (summer) 🚎 Trolleybus: 1, 2, 3, 6) you'll find lots of reading matter, but there's also a permanent exhibition of graphic artist Eduard Wiiralt's work. The Soviet architecture itself is interesting. The **Tallinn Art Hall Foundation** (see page 86) has some very daring art inside the conservative walls of its 1930s building. The smaller exhibition in the Hall is always free, but the main gallery can be seen at no charge on the last day of each temporary show.

For a free experience, you can't beat a fair or a festival. During the summer the streets of Old Town come to life during Old Town Days and the Medieval Market when you'll find locals in period costume.

▶ *It costs nothing to browse the Medieval Market*

When it rains

Do as the Estonians do and head for a café to drink coffee and discuss how to solve the problems of the world. Then, once you have had your caffeine fix, you'll have plenty of energy to explore some of the city's museums.

Start with the Linnamuuseum (Tallinn City Museum, see page 80), located in a handsomely restored merchant's house. From medieval costumed figures to posters and photographs, this museum brings the history of Tallinn to life. A bonus is that much of the explanatory text is in English.

Directly across the street from the City Museum is the Dominican Monastery (see page 73), once one of the most powerful institutions in medieval Tallinn. Today, it is home to a comprehensive collection of medieval and Renaissance stone carvings, including some very intricately carved tombstones.

Still need to burn off some of that caffeine? Head to the **Energy Centre** (by the harbour at ⓐ Põhja pst. 29 ⓛ 10.00–17.00) for some hands-on experiences with technology. This museum is filled with some strange-looking machinery that may leave you wondering about its purpose as not all signs have been translated into English.

If the weather is not only rainy but cold, spend some time in a sauna. Although Estonia's neighbour to the north, Finland, reigns undisputed as the sauna capital of the world, Tallinn does have its fair share of hotspots. There's even a medieval 'Sauna Tower' in Tallinn's Old Town. A lot of hotels and sports clubs in Tallinn have saunas available to rent by the hour. At **Kalma** (ⓐ Vana-Kalamaja 9a ⓞ 627 1811 ⓦ www.bma.ee/kalma), the oldest public bath in Tallinn, a sauna may be taken for between 65–90kr. If you want a more upmarket sweat, try the **Meriton Grand Hotel** (ⓐ Toom pst. 27

667 7000) at 800kr per hour in the evening. Should you drink beer as part of the sauna experience? By all means after you've finished, but not before. Alternatively, take yourself off to one of the day spas in Tallinn or nearby Pirita.

Note that a spa visit in Estonia can involve a bit of pampering, but it may also reveal the true state of your health. If you're not keen to confront that reality, opt for a soothing massage instead.

◆ *There are some hot and steamy venues when it's cold outside*

On arrival

TIME DIFFERENCE

Estonia is two hours ahead of Greenwich Mean Time (GMT),
and three hours ahead during daylight saving.

ARRIVING

By air

With direct flights from 23 cities, Tallinn is easily accessible by air.
Customs and immigration procedures are usually very quick.

Tallinn's airport is small and uncrowded. It is located just 3 km
(2 miles) from the city centre and has excellent facilities, including
ATMs, currency exchange, duty free shops, restaurants and tourist
information. Car rental companies are on the ground floor, next to
the entrance to the car park.

From the airport to the city, take bus no. 2, which operates from
07.00–24.00 between the airport, the city centre and the port every
20 mins (every 30 mins Sun), price 15kr. Tickets can be purchased
directly from the bus driver. A taxi from the airport to the city centre
should cost about 70kr.

Tallinn Airport ⓐ Lennujaama tee 2 ⓣ 605 8701
ⓦ www.tallinn-airport.ee ⓥ Bus: 2

By rail

There are regular train services from Russia and Latvia. Local services
run to Tartu and Pärnu, but train travel is not a hugely popular form
of transport in Estonia.

The train station is situated near the Old Town and is about
1 km (0.6 miles) from both the city centre and the harbour. There are
currency exchange booths in the train station and ATMs next to the

front doors. From the train station to the city centre, take trams 1 or 2, or just walk a couple of hundred metres into the Old Town.

Train Station ② Toompuiestee 37 ① 615 6851 ③ Tram: 1, 2; trolleybus: 4, 5, 7; bus: 21, 21B, 59

By road

Tallinn is connected by international bus lines to most major cities in Latvia, Lithuania, Russia, Poland and Germany.

The Tallinn Central Bus Terminal is located 1 km (0.6 miles) from the city centre. There is a cash-only currency exchange at the terminal, but its rates are poor. There is an ATM by the main entrance.

Most incoming buses stop at more central locations, such as Viru väljak, before reaching the main terminal. From the bus station to other parts of the city, take trams 2 or 4, or buses 17, 17A or 23. A taxi to the Old Town should cost about 50kr.

Tallinn Central Bus Terminal ② Lastekodu 46 ① 680 0900 ③ Tram: 2, 4; bus: 2, 15, 39

● *The train from Moscow*

Tallinn is connected to the rest of Europe by two major highways: Highway 1 (E20) goes east to Russia, and Highway 4 (E67) goes south to Latvia. Entering Estonia from Latvia is quite easy, since both countries are now members of the EU. However, entering from Russia can take a bit of time. In both cases, you will need the car's registration papers and proof of insurance. You can also bring a car in by ferry from Finland or Sweden.

IF YOU GET LOST, TRY...

Excuse me, do you speak English?
Vabandage, kas te oskate inglise keelt?
Vah-ban-da-ghe, kas teh os-kah-teh ing-li-seh ke-elt?

Excuse me, is this the right way to the Old Town/the city centre/the tourist office/the station/the bus station?
Kuidas minna vanalinna/turismiinfosse/raudteejaama/bussijaama?
Kuy-das minnah va-nah-lee-nah/ toor-eess-meen-fosser/ rowd-te-eh-ya-a-mah/pussy-ya-a-mah?

Can you point to it on my map?
Kas te võite näidata, kus see on kaardi peal?
Kas teh voy-teh nay-da-tah, kus se-e on ka-ar-di pe-al?

I am looking for this address	**I am looking for the . . . hotel**
Ma otsin seda aadressi	Palun, kus on hotell . . .
Mah ot-sin seh-da a-ad-res-sy	*Pah-loon, kus on hot-tel . . .*

In Estonia, as in the rest of continental Europe, the traffic drives on the right-hand side of the road. Estonian law requires an international driver's licence and a valid insurance policy. During daylight hours, dipped headlights or daytime running lights must be used. After dark, the main headlights must be switched on. The driver and the passengers must wear seat belts at all times. Petrol stations are easy to find. The largest international chains operating in Estonia are Statoil and Neste.

Both major highways take you right to the centre of town. Traffic is light compared to many cities, so driving into town is easy.

Parking in the city centre and the Old Town area must be paid for, although the first 15 minutes of parking are free. A valid parking ticket must be displayed in your windscreen from 07.00–19.00 on weekdays and 08.00–15.00 on Saturdays in the city centre. In the Old Town, parking must be paid for 24 hours a day. Tickets are sold by special guards. Guarded and indoor car parks are also available.

By water
Ferries and catamarans arrive from Finland and Sweden at the passenger port, which is less than 1 km (0.6 miles) from the centre of town and has currency exchange booths and ATMs. A taxi from the port to the centre of town should cost about 40kr.

Buses 90 and 92 stop here, and can take you into town. The cost is 15Kr and tickets are available from the driver. A taxi from the port to the centre of town should cost about 40kr.

FINDING YOUR FEET
Traffic in Tallinn is light compared to other large cities, but the driving tends to be aggressive and definitely not pedestrian friendly.

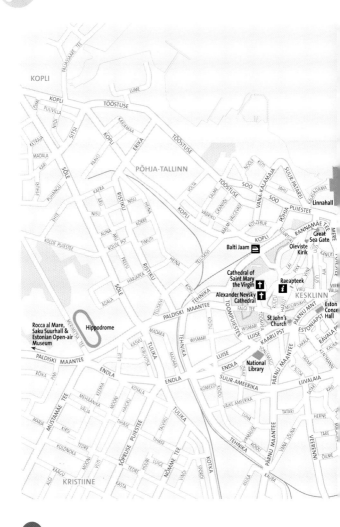

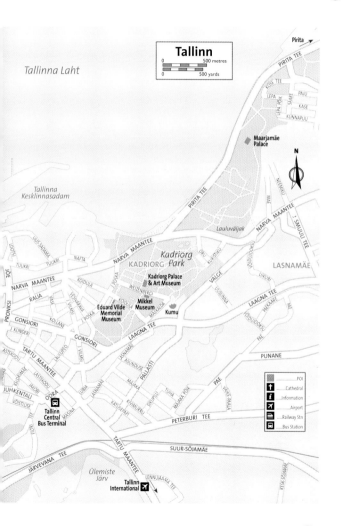

Tallinn

| 0 | 500 metres |
| 0 | 500 yards |

Tallinna Laht

Pirita

PIRITA TEE

KÖSE TEE

LEPA

LEPA PÕIK

PAJU

KASE

KÜNNAPUU

Maarjamäe
Palace

N

*Tallinna
Kesklinnasadam*

PIRITA TEE

NEEMRKU

MÄE

NARVA MAANTEE

J. SMUULI TEE

Lauluväljak

NARVA MAANTEE

POSKA

*Kadriorg
Park*

ORU

KUVÕTKU

TÕNISMÄGI

KADRIORG

Kadriorg Palace
& Art Museum

WEIZENBERGI

VALGE

LASNAMÄE

LIIKURI

LOOTSI

UUS-SADAMA

TUUKRI

TUUKRI

NAFTA

KOIDULA

VESIVÄRAVA

J. VILMSI

POSKA

KOIDULA

KOTZEBUE

UUSLINNA

Eduard Vilde
Memorial
Museum

Mikkel
Museum

Kumu

MAISALU

LAAGNA TEE

PAEKAARE

PAE

JÕE

NARVA MAANTEE

PRONKSI

RAUA

VASE

J. VILMSI

KOLLANE

LAAGNA TEE

KÕDUJOOKSU

GONSIORI

J. KUNDERI

GONSIORI

VILMSI

MAJAKA

ASUNDUSE

PALLASTI

PAE

PUNANE

TARTU MAANTEE

ASTEKODU

KELDRIMÄE

ASTEKODU

JAGODI

LASNAMÄE

LUBJA

MAJAKA PÕIK

TUHA

MAJAKA

VÄIKE PAALA

JUHKENTALI

VÕISTLUSE

ODRA

MAGASINI

KÕRBJA

KIVIMURRU

KATUSEPAPI

Tallinn
Central
Bus Terminal

PETERBURI TEE

PALLASTI

SUUR-SÕJAMÄE

KESK-SÕJAMÄE

JÄRVEVANA TEE

TARTU MAANTEE

*Ülemiste
Järv*

LENNUJAA-KA TEE

Tallinn
International ✈

	POI
🕆	Cathedral
ℹ	Information
✈	Airport
🚆	Railway Stn
🚌	Bus Station

Foreign visitors are especially vulnerable and should take extra precautions at intersections.

Although the overall crime rate is low, petty theft is a problem, especially from cars. Stealing from hotel rooms, especially the cheaper ones, is not uncommon. Sneak thieves and pickpockets are less prevalent than in Western European cities, but do represent a problem. Visitors would be well advised not to carry large sums of cash, and not to flaunt expensive jewellery, cameras or electronic equipment. Such items are better left at home unless really needed. Tallinn also has its share of muggers, so beware of areas that are not well lit, or derelict in appearance, especially at night and near drinking establishments. If possible, do not walk alone.

● Tallinn's city centre is compact and quaint

The exception to normal city life is the Old Town. Here, the narrow winding streets are not conducive to cars, and few are present, with the exception of early morning hours when the Old Town is full of aggressive delivery drivers. With most of the Old Town reserved for pedestrians, everything seems to run at a much more leisurely and relaxed pace.

The best deal in town is a Tallinn Card (available for 6, 24, 48 or 72 hours, ranging from 130–450kr.), which, for a reasonable price, gives you access to most museums, attractions, public transport and discounts on other entertainment.

English is quite commonly spoken in Estonia, and more and more Estonians, especially those in international business and the tourist industry, are learning it. There is one English-language newspaper in Estonia: the *Baltic Times* is published weekly and is available at most hotels, some restaurants and many news-stands. Other English-language publications are shipped into Tallinn, and again, are available at most major hotels, and at many news-stands.

ORIENTATION

Tallinn sits on a bay in the Gulf of Finland, about 85 km (52 miles) south of Helsinki. The historic heart of Tallinn, the Old Town, is about 1.2 km (1 mile) long by about 1 km (0.6 mile) wide. It sits on a hill overlooking the bay, and for the most part is surrounded by defensive walls built in medieval times.

The skyline of the Old Town is dominated by the spires of several churches and the turrets of Toompea Castle. Raekoja plats (Town Hall Square) is virtually in the geographic centre of the Old Town. The streets of the Old Town radiate outward from Town Hall Square in a rather haphazard fashion.

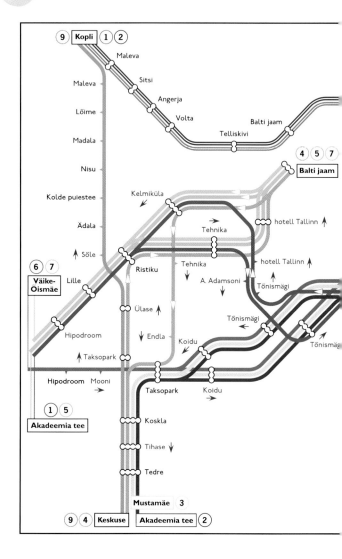

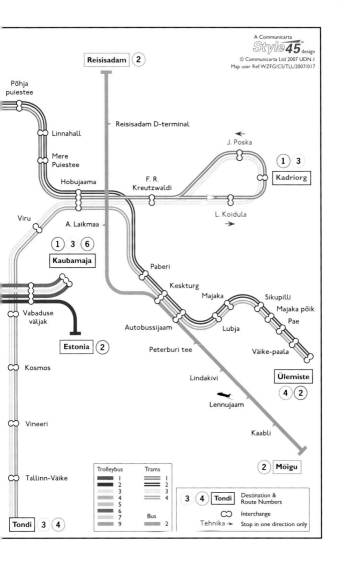

The main railway station is at the northwest foot of the Old Town, and a short 200 m (660 ft) walk, albeit uphill, puts you inside the Old Town. The main international bus terminal is about 1 km (0.6 miles) southeast of the Old Town, with regular local bus services directly to the Old Town.

The rest of the 'new' city radiates eastward and westward from the Old Town. A few kilometres east is the suburb of Pirita (see page 96), while about 6 km (3.5 miles) west is the upmarket suburb of Rocca al Mare, home to the Estonian Open-air Museum (see page 94).

GETTING AROUND

Tallinn is a fairly small, compact city, so getting around is quite easy. The centre of town is Viru väljak. It is at the foot of the hill, or dome, upon which Toompea and the Old Town are built, and is also the junction of Highway 1 (Narva Maantee) from the east, and Highway 4 (Pärnu Maantee) from the south.

Toompea, which is built on the top of the hill that dominates Tallinn, is the main city landmark, and easily seen from anywhere in the city. If you get lost, just head for the hill to get your bearings.

Many of the points of interest are within 1 km (0.6 miles) of Viru väljak, and most are within 2 km (just over a mile). As the city is so pedestrian-friendly, walking is the best way to see certain parts of it, which is why some addresses in this guide have no public transport information.

Taxis are also available, but be warned that some drivers are less than scrupulous. Make sure that the taxi has a visible meter, that it works, and that the driver starts it. The driver should also have his registration, complete with photograph and stamps, prominently displayed. The cost of a taxi from one point to another within the city centre should be no more than 80kr. It is always a good idea to

⬥ *Trams are another way of getting around in Tallinn*

ask your driver for a receipt. If you suspect you were dealt with dishonestly, your hotel receptionist can check your receipt to make sure the distance travelled matches your fare. Quality hotels have clout with the taxi companies, and over-charged passengers can and do receive refunds.

CAR HIRE

Unless you are going to visit locations outside of Tallinn, renting a car is not recommended. The city is compact enough, with most of the attractions close enough, that walking, using the public transport, or even hiring taxis, is much more economical and practical. Also, parking spaces are hard to find, and expensive. Most of the major car rental agencies are represented in Tallinn, both at the airport, and in the city centre. You can expect to pay the same prices as in Western Europe. There are some local car rental companies that can be cheaper than the major ones, but the mechanical condition of the car may be questionable.

Some major car rental agencies are:

Avis ⓐ Liivalaia 13/15 ⓣ 667 1500 ⓛ 08.00–17.00 Mon–Fri, closed Sat & Sun ⓦ www.avis.ee

Budget ⓐ Tallinn Airport ⓣ 605 8600 ⓛ 09.00–18.00 ⓦ www.budget.ee

Europcar ⓐ Tallinn Airport ⓣ 605 8031 ⓛ 09.00–18.00 ⓦ www.europcar.ee

Hertz ⓐ Tallinn Airport ⓣ 605 8923 ⓛ 09.00–18.00 ⓦ www.hertz.ee

National ⓐ Tallinn Airport ⓣ 605 8071 ⓛ 09.00–18.00 ⓦ www.nationalcar.ee

◐ *Raekoja plats – Town Hall Square – is at the heart of the city*

The Old Town

Tallinn has had a turbulent past. Much of the time the city has either been under siege or lived with the threat of invasion. To cope, the residents built massive walls to surround the town. With some 46 towers, medieval Tallinn was possibly the most fortified town in all of Northern Europe. Today, only 20 towers and nearly 2 km (1.5 miles) of the walls remain. A few of the towers, such as Fat Margaret and Kiek in de Kök (Peep into the Kitchen), serve as museums, while many others have been transformed into restaurants, hotels, homes and offices. The oldest of the towers, Nunne, Sauna and Kuldjala, remain open to the public.

The Old Town may appear compact on the map, but you can spend hours, if not days, exploring its intriguing nooks and crannies. Your adventure on foot will give you a glimpse of life in Tallinn. From up-and-coming entrepreneurs who can afford to renovate ancient buildings, to the ageing ladies who come to beg outside the Lutheran cathedral, the Old Town is a mix of the Tallinn of yesterday and today.

The joy of sightseeing in the Old Town area of Tallinn is that it is comfortably walkable. The narrow, twisted, and sometimes quite vertically inclined streets allow for minimal car traffic, and no public transport.

SIGHTS & ATTRACTIONS

Alexander Nevsky Cathedral

Built in 1900, this relative newcomer does not quite fit architecturally into the rest of the medieval Old Town. A typical onion-domed Russian Orthodox Church, it sits next to the Toompea Castle and can be seen from most parts of the city. Inside is an impressive

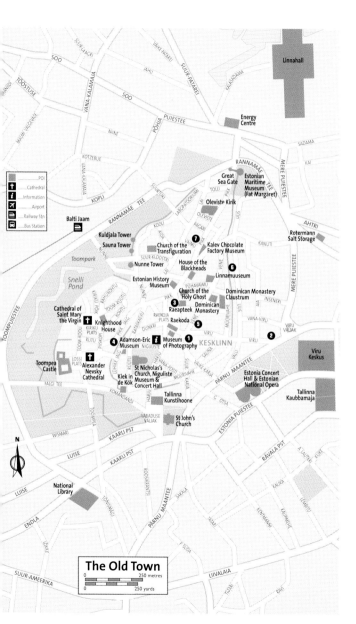

The Old Town

	POI
	Cathedral
	Information
	Airport
	Railway Stn
	Bus Station

Linnahall

Energy Centre

Great Sea Gate

Estonian Maritime Museum (Fat Margaret)

Oleviste Kirik

Rotermann Salt Storage

Balti Jaam

Kuldjala Tower

Sauna Tower

Church of the Transfiguration

Kalev Chocolate Factory Museum

Nunne Tower

House of the Blackheads

Estonian History Museum

Linnamuseum

Church of the Holy Ghost

Dominican Monastery Claustrum

Raeapteek

Dominican Monastery

Cathedral of Saint Mary the Virgin

Knighthood House

Raekoda

Adamson-Eric Museum

Museum of Photography

KESKLINN

Toompea Castle

Alexander Nevsky Cathedral

Kiek in de Kök

St Nicholas's Church, Niguliste Museum & Concert Hall

Tallinna Kunstihoone

Viru Keskus

Estonia Concert Hall & Estonian National Opera

Tallinna Kaubamaja

St John's Church

National Library

Toompark

Snelli Pond

0   250 metres

0   250 yards

A SPOT OF BOTHER
Look for two long cobblestones that form the letter 'L' in a corner of Town Hall Square near the Raeapteek. This marks the location where a priest was beheaded, on the spot, for having killed a waitress who brought food not to his liking. The moral: don't enter the priesthood until you've worked through your anger issues.

display of religious icons. ❸ Lossi plats 10 ❶ 644 3484 ❸ 08.00–19.00 ❼ www.hot.ee/nsobor

Church of the Holy Ghost
Built in the 1360s, this historic church is the only one in Tallinn with an original exterior. The clock, set into the wall in 1680, is the oldest timepiece in Estonia. Although simple and humble on the outside, the interior is richly decorated and contains precious works of medieval art. ❸ Pühavaimu 2 ❶ 646 4430 ❸ 10.00–15.00 Mon–Sat, closed Sun (summer); 10.00–15.00 Mon–Fri, closed Sat & Sun (winter)

Church of the Transfiguration
Originally belonging to St Michael's Convent of the Cistercian Order (located next door and now housing the Gustavus Adolphus School), the church was given to an Orthodox congregation in 1716. The church has retained its original form, aside from the addition of a baroque spire in 1776 and exterior renovations in the early 1800s. The carved-wood iconostasis is one of the most impressive of its kind. ❸ Suur-Kloostri 14-1 ❶ 646 4003

⬣ The cathedral illustrates Russian influence on the country

Dominican Monastery

One of Tallinn's oldest existing buildings, this monastery was founded in 1246. The part of the monastery administered by the museum includes the courtyard and surrounding passageways, where fascinating 15th- and 16th-century stone carvings are on display. To see the inner rooms, visit the Claustrum, listed below. ❷ Vene 16 ❶ 644 4606 Ⓦ www.kloostri.ee ⏱ 10.00–18.00. Admission charge

Dominican Monastery Claustrum

The monastery's inner chambers, including the monk's dormitory, priory and library, can only be visited as part of an organised tour (the entrance is around the corner, which is why it's in a different street). One of the most interesting spots is the downstairs room that houses the 'energy pillar', said to be the source of a mysterious power. ❷ Müürivahe 33 ❶ 644 6530 Ⓦ www.mauritanum.edu.ee ⏱ 10.00–17.00. Admission charge

Estonian History Museum

Housed in the Great Guild Hall, the museum's exhibitions cover Estonia's earliest history up to the 18th century, with explanations translated into English. The building itself was a gathering place for Tallinn's wealthy merchants. ❷ Pikk 17 ❶ 641 1630 Ⓦ www.eam.ee ⏱ 11.00–18.00 Thur–Tues, closed Wed. Admission charge

Estonian Maritime Museum

Tallinn's significant seafaring history is put on display in this museum housed over four floors of the 16th-century Fat Margaret tower. Don't miss the antique diving equipment or the spectacular views

◀ *House of the Blackheads*

from the roof. ⓐ Pikk 70 ⓘ 641 1408 ⓦ www.meremuuseum.ee
ⓗ 10.00–18.00 Wed–Sun, closed Mon & Tues Admission charge

Great Sea Gate

At the northern end of the Old Town, the Great Sea Gate is
a 16th-century arch flanked by two towers. The larger of the two towers
is Fat Margaret, a barrel-shaped tower whose walls are 4 m (13 ft) thick.
When it was no longer needed for defensive purposes, it became the
city's jail. Today, it houses the Estonian Maritime Museum. ⓐ Pikk 70
ⓘ 641 1408 ⓗ 10.00–18.00 Wed–Sun, closed public holidays

House of the Blackheads

The Brotherhood of the Blackheads was a merchants' guild founded
in 1343, and the house was built as lodgings for visiting merchants.
Over the centuries it evolved into a social drinking club, finally
dissolving in 1940 when the Russians moved in. The house is
elaborately decorated in Renaissance style, both inside and out.
It's not normally open to the public, but you can see the interior
if you attend one of the regular chamber concerts. ⓐ Pikk 26
ⓘ 631 3199 ⓦ www.mustpeademaja.ee

Kiek in de Kök (Peep into the Kitchen)

This combination tower and museum provides an excellent introduction
to the history of Tallinn's elaborate defence system of walls and towers.
Three floors of the tower, restored to its 17th-century appearance,
contain galleries showing contemporary art. The unusual name comes
from the vantage point it offers if you climb to the top of its stairs.

▶ *It is easy to spot which of the towers is Fat Margaret*

ⓐ Komandandi 2 ⓣ 644 6686 ⓦ www.linnamuuseum.ee/kok
ⓛ 10.30–18.00 Tues–Sun, closed Mon

Oleviste Kirik (St Olaf's Church)
The spire of this church is Tallinn's landmark and at one time it may
have been the tallest spire in the whole of Europe. Although the
church dates from 1267, the interior is from the 1840s. ⓐ Lai tn. 50
ⓣ 641 2241 ⓦ www.oleviste.ee ⓛ 10.00–14.00 Tues–Fri, closed
Sat–Mon

Raeapteek (Town Hall Pharmacy)
One of the oldest continuously running pharmacies in Europe
is on Town Hall Square. Records exist showing it dates back
to at least 1422, but it may have opened even earlier than that.
In medieval times the ailing could buy burnt bees and bat powder
for treatments, and if you didn't have a specific illness you could
buy a glass of spiced claret. The pharmacy offers modern
medications these days, and part of the store is a museum.
ⓐ Raekoja plats 11 ⓣ 631 4860 ⓛ 09.00–19.00 Mon–Fri,
09.00–17.00 Sat, 09.00–16.00 Sun

Raekoda & Raekoja plats (Town Hall & Town Hall Square)
Town Hall Square is as old as Tallinn itself. Surrounded by medieval
buildings painted in pastel colours, the square is an Estonian
landmark, and a popular rallying point for Estonian patriotism.
On the south side stands the Town Hall, built in the 15th century.
Look up to see the Gothic arches, steeple and weather vane. Note
the water-spouting green painted dragons just below the roof line.
ⓐ Raekoja plats 1 ⓣ 645 7900 ⓦ www.tallinn.ee/raekoda

St John's Church

A pseudo-Gothic church built for a local Lutheran congregation, St John's boasts the first bell (dating from 1872) inscribed in Estonian. ⓐ Vabaduse väljak 1 ⓘ 644 6206 ⓒ 10.00–14.00 Tues, Thur & Fri, 10.00–17.00 Wed, closed Mon & Sat, Services 10.00 Sun ⓝ Tram: 3, 4; bus: 5, 14, 18, 20, 20A, 36

St Nicholas's Church

Started in the 13th century and rebuilt in the 15th century, this imposing church is now a museum housing Tallinn's collection of medieval art. There are several carved and painted altars, friezes, tomb-top effigies, and other interesting works. The present classical building dates from the 1820s, but a Russian Orthodox church stood here in

BOY OF BRONZE

Originally erected in 1947, this monument of a Red Army soldier used to stand in front of the National Library. It has always inspired controversy: to some, it represented the liberation of Estonia from the Nazis by Soviet forces; to others, it came to symbolise Soviet repression. In April 2007, the Estonian government decided to move the statue to a new location at the military cemetery. Young people, mostly Russian-speakers, flocked to the site and rioted for two nights surrounding its removal. Eventually, after a handbags-at-dawn propaganda battle with Russia, things settled down and the Russian-speaking population is now getting used to the statue's new location (ⓐ Filtri tee 14 ⓝ Bus: 13).

the early 1400s. The young church houses many objects of artistic value predating it, including 16th-century icons. ⓐ Niguliste 3 ⓕ 631 4330 ⓒ 10.00–17.00 Wed–Sun, closed Mon & Tues, Services 09.30 & 18.00 Sat, 10.00 Sun

Toompea Castle

Sitting at the very top of Toompea, the hill that overlooks the city, this castle has guarded Tallinn for most of its history. It was an Estonian stockade until it was captured in 1219 by the Danes, who built the first stone castle. Over the centuries, the castle has been rebuilt and renovated many times; the latest refurbishment was by Russia's Catherine the Great, who gave it its pink baroque façade. It is dominated by three defensive towers, the tallest of which, Tall Herman, dates from 1371. ⓐ Lossi plats ⓘ Admission only with guided tour

CULTURE

To find out what's on and to book tickets, see ⓦ www.concert.ee

Adamson-Eric Museum

The permanent collection of works by world-famous artist Adamson-Eric is housed in a 16th-century building within the Old Town. ⓐ Lühike jalg 3 ⓕ 644 5838 ⓒ 11.00–18.00 Wed–Sun, closed Mon & Tues. Admission charge (free with Tallinn Card)

Estonia Concert Hall

The number one place to hear classical music and operatic performances. ⓐ Estonia pst. 4 ⓕ 614 7760 ⓝ Tram: 2; bus: 3, 9, 11, 14, 15, 16, 17A, 18, 20, 23, 23A, 40, 48

🔺 *Toompea Castle looms tall over Tallinn*

Estonian National Opera

This company has its home at the Estonia Concert Hall. ② Estonia pst. 4
① 683 1201 Ⓜ Tram: 2; bus: 3, 9, 11, 14, 15, 16, 17A, 18, 20, 23, 23A, 40, 48

House of the Blackheads

This gloriously ornate guildhall (see page 74) stages classical music
concerts nearly every night. It also hosts monthly social dances, so
be sure to get a copy of the events calendar. ② Pikk 26 ① 631 3199

Knighthood House

This grand building perched on Toompea Hill serves as the main
branch of the Art Museum of Estonia. The collection provides an
excellent overview of Estonian art. ② Kiriku plats 1 ① 644 9340
🕓 11.00–18.00 Wed–Sun, closed Mon & Tues. Admission charge

Linnamuuseum (Tallinn City Museum)

Housed in a 14th-century merchant house, this museum manages
to compact centuries of the city's history into a complete and
lively array of exhibits. Most of the exhibits have English captions.
② Vene 17 ① 644 6553 Ⓦ www.linnamuuseum.ee 🕓 10.30–18.00
Wed–Mon, closed Tues

Museum of Photography

Nowadays, the former city prison, which dates from the 14th century,
houses a compact exhibition on Estonian photography. The first
camera arrived in Tallinn just one year after debuting in France and
the art developed quickly here. Don't miss the contemporary
exhibitions and shop. ② City Prison, Raekoja tn. 4/6 ① 644 8767
Ⓦ www.linnamuuseum.ee 🕓 10.30–18.00 Thur–Tues, closed Wed.
Admission charge (free with Tallinn Card)

Niguliste Museum & Concert Hall
This 13th-century Gothic church, which houses a fascinating collection of medieval art, holds regular organ concerts.
ⓐ Niguliste 3 ⓣ 631 4340

RETAIL THERAPY

In retail terms, Tallinn doesn't just offer itself on a plate. You have to look a little to find the city's shopping possibilities, but of course there's a thrill in that chase.

If you are looking for a special souvenir, the streets of the Old Town are the place to go. Linen, wool clothing and amber jewellery are local specialities, and you will find these at many shops, especially along Pikk and Dunkri. The best place for knitted gems is the open-air woollen market on Müürivahe just north of Viru Gate.

Most stores are open Mon–Fri from 10.00–17.00. Shops close early on Saturday and may not open at all on Sunday. However, since this is a prime area for tourists you're likely to find a good selection of shops that can't resist catering to visitors.

SPECIALITY & SOUVENIR SHOPS

Antiik This charming outlet offers a wide range of old – and even antique – objects that make really classy gifts and souvenirs.
ⓐ Kinga 5 ⓣ 646 6232 ⓦ www.antiqueshop.ee

Apollo Bookstore Lots of novels and guidebooks in English.
ⓐ Viru 23 ⓝ Tram: 3, 4; bus: 5, 14, 18, 20, 20A, 36, 40, 48

Draakoni Gallery This quaint gallery also houses a shop where you can buy works of art. ⓐ Pikk 18 ⓣ 646 4110

● Flowers aren't just saved for special occasions

Katariina Guild A collection of several craft workshops along Catherine's passage, selling ceramics, leatherwork, stained glass and jewellery. ⓐ Katariina Käik ① 641 8054

Lino Great selection of knits and linens. ⓐ Pikk 12 ① 646 4474

Madeli Käsitöö This is a fabulous place to go if you're looking for authentically regional souvenirs of your stay. No tat. ⓐ Väike-Karja ① 620 9272

Sepa Äri Products of Estonia's long tradition of smithing. ⓐ Olevimägi 11 ① 680 0971

Veta Probably the best linens in town. The tablecloths and clothes, in particular, are excellent. ⓐ Pikk 4 ① 646 4140

Zizi Ethnographic textiles for the home. ⓐ Vene 12 ① 644 1222

TAKING A BREAK

Elsebet £ ❶ Eat in, or take away some of the best pastries in Tallinn. Since your bag of goodies probably won't make it back to the hotel, take a seat at one of the candle-lit wooden tables. ⓐ Viru 2/Vanaturu 6 ① 646 6800 ⓦ www.peppersack.ee ① 08.00–24.00 Mon–Sat, 10.00–23.00 Sun

Hesburger £ ❷ An outpost of the Finnish hamburger chain. ⓐ Viru 27 ① 627 2516 ① 09.00–23.00 Mon–Fri, 09.00–01.00 Sat ⓝ Tram: 3, 4; bus: 5, 14, 18, 20, 20A, 36, 40, 48

Kehrwieder £ ❸ Wonderful pastries right on Town Hall Square, plus its own sandwich shop right across the ancient passage. Among the friendliest service in town. ⓐ Saiakang 1 ⓦ www.kehrwieder.ee ⓒ 11.00–24.00

Bogapott ££ ❹ Hidden away in a part of the medieval town wall on Toompea is this café selling pastries and sandwiches. It doubles as an art shop with a ceramics studio. ⓐ Pikk jalg 9 ⓣ 631 3181 ⓦ www.bogapott.ee ⓒ 10.00–18.00

Chocolaterie Café ££ ❺ Quaint, pretty and in need of a lot more chairs. A master *chocolatier* makes truffles from scratch. Just the sugar hit you'll need to carry on sightseeing. ⓐ Vene 6 (in the courtyard) ⓣ 641 8061 ⓒ 10.00–22.00

Kibuvits ££ ❻ Good spot to have lunch or just kick back and read the paper. ⓐ Uus 19 ⓣ 641 2096 ⓒ 10.00–21.00

Le Bonaparte £££ ❼ This is an ideal café to grab a coffee and pastry in the middle of the day. ⓐ Pikk 45/47 ⓣ 646 4444 ⓒ 08.00–20.00 Mon–Sat, 10.00–18.00 Sun

AFTER DARK

BARS & CLUBS
Guitar Safari If you want to hear rock and blues in a calm, appreciative atmosphere, this is your place. ⓐ Müürivahe 22 ⓣ 641 1607 ⓦ www.guitarsafari.ee ⓒ 12.00–01.00 Mon–Fri & Sun, 14.00–03.00 Sat

Karoliina Shaped like a tunnel and dug into a hillside of the Old Town, this is a great place for quiet and cosy conversation. Try the spiked mulled wine. ❸ Harju 6 🕐 11.00–22.00

Kompressor Students love the simple décor, oversized tables and cheap drinks here. Add to that the good and incredibly cheap pancakes, and you've got the makings of a budget night out. ❸ Rataskaevu 3 🕿 646 4210 🕐 11.00–23.00 Mon–Thur, 11.00–02.00 Fri–Sun

Rock Café Built into a giant stone-walled paper factory on Tartu maantee, this is the country's hottest destination for live music. International acts and top locals play here. The owner is also a morning show DJ, and he's in the club nightly to make sure it's run right. ❸ Tartu mnt. 8od, Third Floor 🌐 www.rockcafe.ee 🕐 21.00–04.00 Thur, 22.00–04.00 Fri–Sun, closed Mon–Wed

St Patrick's Irish of vibe, Estonian of customer base. The food is good and every fourth Saku Originaal is free. ❸ Suur-Karja 8 🕿 641 8173 🌐 www.patricks.ee 🕐 11.00–02.00 Sun–Thur, 11.00–04.00 Fri & Sat

Valli Baar At first glance this Old Town pub doesn't look worthy of a second glance. But at night, when students drop in for cheap drinks and elderly regulars start to swing to the live accordion music, the atmosphere moves into the realm of the surreal. ❸ Müürivahe 14 🕿 641 8379 🕐 11.00–23.00

Von Krahli Baar If you don't dig alternative bands in a studenty atmosphere, then at least stop by for the cheap, good food during the day. ❸ Rataskaevu 10/12 🕿 626 9096 🌐 www.vonkrahl.ee 🕐 12.00–01.00 Mon–Thur, 12.00–03.00 Fri & Sat, closed Sun

City Centre

Although most visitors don't venture outside it, there is much more to Tallinn than its Old Town. Once outside of that compact area, you'll discover a modern city humming with activity and populated with familiar global signage from Radisson to TGI Friday's. Once again, public transport can sometimes be either unavailable or not worth missing a lovely walk for; we've included it wherever it's a realistic option. As with all contemporary cities, the focus is more on business than sightseeing, but there are more than enough galleries and museums to keep your interest level high.

CULTURE

Linnahall

This great grey monolith at the edge of the harbour plays host to pop concerts and big-name artists. ❸ Mere pst. 20 ❶ 641 1500 Ⓝ Tram: 1, 2; bus: 3

Saku Suurhall

This concert and sports arena is best known for having hosted the Eurovision Song Contest in 2002. The venue holds a range of events and has its own sports bar and restaurant. ❸ Paldiski mnt. 104 ❶ 660 0200 Ⓦ www.sakuarena.com Ⓝ Trolleybus: 6, 7; bus: 21, 22

Tallinna Kunstihoone (Tallinn Art Hall Foundation)

This imposing 1930s building houses avant-garde and daring exhibitions from Estonia and abroad. ❸ Vabaduse Square 6, 10146 Tallinn ❶ 644 2818 ❶ 12.00–18.00 Wed–Mon, closed Tues Ⓝ Trolleybus: 1, 2, 3, 6; tram: 3, 4

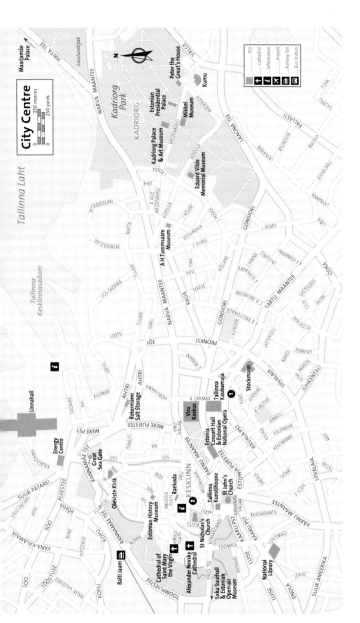

A H TAMMSAARE – ESTONIA'S KAFKA

Anton Hansen Tammsaare (1878–1940) is generally considered to be the greatest Estonian writer of the 20th century. His work is set against a background of – and is infused by – his own experience of almost life-long physical and psychological suffering. His books are exquisitely poignant, and the most famous of them make up the five-part epic *Truth and Justice*. The A H Tammsaare Museum chronicles his life and work (and exhibits his death mask), but just as interesting is the apartment, painstakingly restored to its 1930s original, where he spent his last eight years.
ⓐ L Koidula 12a ❶ 601 3232 Ⓦ www.linnamuuseum.ee/tammsaare ❶ 11.00–17.00 Wed–Sun, closed Mon & Tue
Ⓝ Tram: 1, 3. Admission charge (but free with Tallinn Card)

RETAIL THERAPY

Tallinn is served by three large department stores (the second two of which are connected by a walkway) within walking distance of its Old Town:

Stockmann ⓐ Liivalaia 53
Tallinna Kaubamaja ⓐ Gonsiori 2
Viru Keskus ⓐ Viru väljak 4

Kalev Chocolate Factory Museum This place sells a wide variety of Estonian chocolate, and you can also see marzipan being painted.
ⓐ Pikk 16 ❶ 646 4192

○ Contrasting building styles in the city centre

Lasering Estonian and international rock and pop CDs and DVDs — everything from indie to film soundtracks. ❸ Pärnu mnt. 38 ❶ 627 9279

Rahva Raamat The city's best and biggest bookstore is found on the top floor of the Viru Keskus. It has a large selection of foreign-language books, as well as two popular cafés. ❸ Viru väljak 4 ❶ 610 1444

AFTER DARK

RESTAURANTS

Lounge 24 £££ ❶ Named for its location on the 24th floor of the Radisson SAS hotel, this is the place to come for a view. The menu is limited, the service is generally good, and the vista always without rival. ❸ Rävala pst. 3 ❶ 682 3424 Ⓦ www.madissoni.ee ❶ 12.00–02.00 Ⓝ Trolleybus: 1, 3, 6

Pegasus £££ ❷ Upstairs is a fine-dining restaurant; downstairs is a café teeming with life. If you're a travelling without family, this is one of the better places to have a nibble. Check the website for information on live jazz nights. ❸ Harju 1 ❶ 631 4040 Ⓦ www.restoranpegasus.ee

PUBS & CLUBS

The Englishman Pub Serving English beer and playing English music, this is not bad at all for a hotel pub. The décor is a cross between a cricket museum and a gentlemen's club, with English newspapers and magazines available, but that doesn't stop the nightlife becoming downright raucous. ❸ Reval Hotel Olümpia, Liivalaia 33 ❶ 631 5831 Ⓦ www.revalhotels.com ❶ 16.00–01.00 Sun–Thur, 16.00–03.00 Fri & Sat

Ice Bar This bar is named for its shot glasses made of ice. The later you go, the more the music picks up, but it's an excellent venue to meet up before setting out on a night on the town. ⊜ Dunkri 6 ⓘ 697 7509 ⓦ www.icebar.ee ⓛ 09.00–24.00 Fri & Sat, 09.00–02.00 Sun–Thur

Kaheksa Kaheksa, meaning the number eight in Estonian, may be the ultimate Estonian lounge. At night it's hopping, and in the day it has some of the best outdoor dining (weather permitting), as well as a smoking room and outstanding food. ⊜ Vana-posti 8 ⓘ 631 4812 ⓦ www.lounge8.ee ⓛ 11.00–23.00 Sun–Fri, 11.00–01.00 Sat

⊙ *The sports bar at Saku Suurhall (see page 86)*

Suburbs East & West

KADRIORG

Kadriorg is a large public park about 1 km (0.6 mile) east of the Old Town. Created by Tsar Peter the Great in the early 18th century, the heavily forested park is criss-crossed with paths, and dotted with statues, ponds and fountains. In the centre is the magnificent Kadriorg Palace. The park contains other historic and important buildings, such as Peter the Great's House, the Estonian Presidential Palace, and several other museums.

SIGHTS & ATTRACTIONS
Kadriorg Palace
Peter I began building the palace in 1718, named Ekaterinenthal, or Catherinenthal, in honour of Catherine I. Currently, the baroque Kadriorg Palace houses the **Kadriorg Art Museum**, the foreign art collection of the Estonian Art Museum. The collection contains more than 900 Western European and Russian paintings from the 16th to the 20th centuries, about 3,500 prints, over 3,000 sculptures and gems, and about 1,600 decorative arts objects (historical furniture, porcelain, glass, etc.). The upper flower garden, behind the palace, has been reconstructed in 18th-century style, and is open to visitors in the summer. The café and museum shop are open during museum opening hours. ③ Weizenbergi 37 ❶ 606 6400 ◷ 10.00–18.00 Tues–Sun (summer); 10.00–17.00 Tues–Sun (winter) ◷ From the city centre, take tram 1 or 3 to the final stop where it is a few minutes' walk to the palace

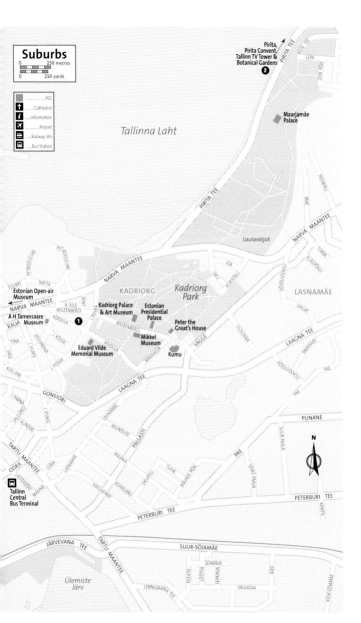

Suburbs

0 ——— 250 metres
0 ——— 250 yards

- ▩ ....POI
- 🕇 ....Cathedral
- 🈘 ....Information
- ✈ ....Airport
- 🚉 ....Railway Stn
- 🚌 ....Bus Station

Pirita,
Pirita Convent,
Tallinn TV Tower &
Botanical Gardens ❷

LEPA

PIRITA TEE

KOSE TEE

LEPA PÕIK

Maarjamäe
Palace

Tallinna Laht

NEHATU

PIRITA TEE

MÄE

NARVA MAANTEE

TURBA

KÜRENÕLU

NARVA MAANTEE

Laulaväljak

IOA

OKI

KÜNSTIKU

KADRIORG

*Kadriorg
Park*

GORDIÕTÕDA

UÜRI

LASNAMÄE

Estonian Open-air
Museum

NARVA MAANTEE

A H Tammsaare
Museum

RAUA

TÜÜRI

PETROOLEUMI

NAFTA

A ALLE
WEIZENBERGI

KOIDULA

LAHE

POSKA

Kadriorg Palace
& Art Museum

WEIZENBERGI

Estonian
Presidential
Palace

Peter the
Great's House

❶

VALGE

USSINKA

LAAGNA TEE

PÄÄSKÜRU

PÕIDÜJÕÕKU

PAE

Eduard Vilde
Memorial Museum

KOIDULA

Mikkel
Museum

MAEKALDA

Kumu

KÖLERI

VESKIARBA

TINA

VAASE

VILMSI

J PÄRNA

KÕLLANE

GONSIORI

J PÄRNA

LALLÜRÜ

KUNDERI

VILMSI

LAAGNA TEE

LASKMAT

ASUNDUSE

PALLASTI

LASNAMÄE

MALAKA

TARTU MAANTEE

ODRA

MASNA

LUBJA

LASNAMÄE

SIKUPILLI

TUHA

MALAKA PÕIK

PAE

VÄIKE PAALA

SUUR PAALA

PUNANE

LATTEOKU

Tallinn
Central
Bus Terminal

KATUSEPAN

KIVIMURRU

PETERBURI TEE

JÄRVEVANA TEE

TARTU MAANTEE

PETERBURI TEE

KAATSI

SUUR-SÕJAMÄE

SEPAPALJA

KEEVISE

LOOTSA

SEPAPAJA

ÄÄSI

*Ülemiste
Järv*

LENNUJAAMA TEE

VALUKOJA

KESK-SÕJAMÄE

N

Kadriorg Park

Only a small part of the large Kadriorg Park was designed as a formal park in its time – most of it was intended to preserve the look of the natural landscape. Lining the promenade leading from the popular Swan Lake to the palace (Weizenbergi Street) are many of the palace's auxiliary buildings. The restoration workshop of the Estonian Art Museum is located in the palace's guest house and the park pavilion next door. Opposite the palace gates is a small guard house, the palace's kitchen building and ice cellar. 🚊 Tram: 1, 3

Mikkel Museum

Johannes Mikkel donated his substantial collection of Chinese, Russian and European paintings, prints, icons and porcelain to the Estonian

ESTONIAN OPEN-AIR MUSEUM

Located on the western outskirts of Tallinn, this museum brings together over 100 Estonian village buildings from the 18th and 19th centuries. Exhibits illustrate how the villagers lived, and how buildings developed from simple longhouses to more sophisticated farmsteads. There are also watermills and windmills. The Kolu Café serves traditional bean soup and beer. 🏠 Vabaõhumuuseumi tee 12 📞 654 9100 🌐 www.evm.ee 🚌 Bus: 21, 21B from the train station; minibus: 234 from behind the Estonia theatre to Vabaõhumuuseum stop. Admission charge (free with Tallinn Card)

▶ *The home of Peter the Great now houses an art museum*

Art Museum in 1994. The collection is now housed in the renovated kitchen building in the grounds of the Kadriorg Palace. ⓐ Weizenbergi 28 ⓣ 601 5844 ⓛ 10.00–17.00 Wed–Sun, closed Mon & Tues ⓦ Tram: 1, 3 to the final stop, then it's a few minutes' walk to the museum

AFTER DARK
Lydia £££ ❶ Next to Kadriorg Park, this restaurant has live music at the weekend to accompany the fine Estonian dining it offers. ⓐ Koidula 13a ⓣ 626 8990 ⓦ www.lydia.ee ⓛ 12.00–23.00 Mon–Sat, 12.00–19.00 Sun

PIRITA

This seaside suburb is located 6 km (3.5 miles) from Tallinn's city centre. In the early 20th century, Pirita began to develop into a destination for Sunday rides and swimming. Today, it's a great place to spend free time, with its bathing beaches, coastline, pine-forested parks and picturesque Pirita river valley. Tallinn's Botanical Gardens has lands on either side of the Pirita river, near the TV Tower (see page 98). To get to Pirita, take bus 34A or 38 from the main bus stop on the ground floor of Viru Keskus.

SIGHTS & ATTRACTIONS
Botanical Gardens
Located in Pirita, near the TV Tower, the gardens feature virtually every type of tree and plant found in Estonia. The grounds are immaculately kept, and in the centre is a Palm House (where they hold changing exhibitions), a rose garden and an alpine garden. ⓐ Kloostrimetsa tee 52 ⓣ 606 2679 ⓛ Glasshouses 11.00–18.00, Gardens 11.00–18.00 (winter); 11.00–19.00 (summer) ⓦ Bus: 34A or 38 from Viru keskus to Kloostrimetsa stop

Lauluväljak (Song Festival Grounds)

This is where the 'Singing Revolution' (see page 21) began in 1988. The Lauluväljak is comprised of both a huge outdoor arena and a modern indoor concert hall. ❷ Narva mnt. 95 ❶ 611 2100 Ⓜ Bus: 1A, 5, 8, 19, 34A, 35, 38, 44, 51, 60, 63

Pirita Convent

Established in 1407, the church was destroyed in the late 1500s, and only the western limestone gable and side walls remain. In the 17th century, a farmers' cemetery developed in front of the ruins. Apparently, secret underground passageways lead from the convent to the city. ❷ Kloostri tee 9 ❶ 5817 3560 ❶ 09.00–19.00 Mon & Tues Ⓜ Bus: 1, 8, 34A, 38 from Viru keskus to Pirita stop. Admission charge (free with Tallinn Card)

⬤ *St Bridget's Convent is possibly linked to Tallinn by secret passages*

▲ Dusk in Pirita's harbour

Tallinn TV Tower

The 314 m (1,030 ft) TV Tower was built for the 1980 Olympic Games. From 170 m (560 ft) you can get a gorgeous view of the city. For longer gazing, there's a restaurant on the same floor as the observation tower. ⓐ Kloostrimetsa 58a ⓣ 600 5511, Booking 623 8250 ⓦ www.teletorn.ee ⓒ 10.00–24.00 ⓝ Bus: 34A, 38

AFTER DARK

Kalevi Yacht Club ££ ② It has become more expensive over the years, but this yacht club is an ideal place to escape the pace of city cafés. Located on the sea side near the Pirita river bridge, it's great for a bite after touring the Pirita neighbourhood. ⓐ Pirita tee 17 ⓣ 623 9158 ⓒ 11.00–23.00

▶ Seventy per cent of Estonia is coastline, so quick escapes are easy

Pärnu

Pärnu is Estonia's best-known summer resort. The attraction lies in its unpolluted shallow sea bay, which is warm by June, and in its fine, white sandy beaches. Sunbathers started coming here in the 19th century, and they continue to flock here every summer.

Aside from the nightclubs and other party scenes, Pärnu offers museums, theatres and live concerts. Spas and recuperation centres are also important here.

GETTING THERE

By road
Pärnu is accessible by car from central Tallinn – take Pärnu maantee (Highway 4) south for 130 km (80 miles). Regular bus services operate between Tallinn and Pärnu, and the journey takes under two hours.

Located right in the centre, the Tourist Information Centre provides tips and brochures and has a booth at the beach in summer.
Tourist Information Centre ⓐ Rüütli 16 ❶ 447 3000 Ⓦ www.parnu.ee

SIGHTS & ATTRACTIONS

Mini Zoo
This is home to some fabulous snakes, spiders and crocodiles.
ⓐ Akadeemia 1 ❶ 551 6033 Ⓦ www.hot.ee/minizoo ❶ 10.00–18.00 Mon–Fri, 11.00– 20.00 Sat & Sun. Admission charge

Parks
A large part of what makes Pärnu such a relaxing place to visit are its vast, green areas designed for strolling. The most notable of these is

◉ Pärnu's Town Hall is an atmospheric setting for summer events

Pärnu, Tartu & Spas outside Tallinn

0 _____ 40 km
0 _____ 20 miles

Soome Laht

Maar

TALLINN
Tallinn International

Paldiski

Dirhami

Nõva

Riisipere

Kohila

Saku

Kärdla

Vormsi

Turba

Rapla

Kõrgessaare

Hiiumaa

Fra Mare Spa

Rohuküla

Haapsalu

Märjamaa

Kehtra

Käina

Haltermaa

Matsalu National Park

Järvakandi

Emmaste

Lihula

Leisi

Muhu

Kuivastu

Orissaare

Pädaste Manor

Virtsu

Koonga

Pärnu-Jaagupi

Saaremaa

Valjala

Varbla

Pärnu

Soom Natior Pc

GO Spa Hotell

Kuressaare

Tõstamaa

Paikuse

Estonia

Kilingi-Nõmme

Häädemeeste

LATV

N
Loksa
Võsu
Lahemaa National Park
:onian Golf Country Club
Kunda
Kalvi Manor
Saka Cliff Hotel & Spa
Kohtla-Järve
Toila Sanatorium
Kehra
Rakvere
Kiviõli
Jõhvi
Sillamäe
Ahtme
Tapa
Tamsalu
Tudu
Aravete
Väike-Maarja
Iisaku
:oosna-Alliku
Rakke
Avinurme
Vasknarva
Kauksi
Paide
ESTONIA
Türi
Mustvee
Peipsi Järv
RUSSIA
Gdov
Jõgeva
Kallaste
Põltsamaa
Suure-Jaani
Koosa
Emajõgi
Tartu
'iljandi
Puhja
Võrtsjärv
Võnnu
Mustla
Rannu
Räpina
Otepää
Põlva
City
Large Town
Small Town
POI
Motorway
Main Road
Minor Road
Airport
Railway

Koidula Park, adjacent to the downtown area, with its colourful flowerbeds and fountain. Another, Rannapark, is no longer a park as such, but now boasts **Nurmenuku puhkekeskus**, a pony dude ranch for children. ☎ 507 7851 Ⓦ www.nurmenukupk.ee ⌚ 11.00–19.00

Pärnu Museum
This museum covers 11,000 years of local history, from the mid-Stone Age to the present. ⓐ Aia 4 ☎ 443 3231 Ⓦ www.pernau.ee ⌚ 10.00–18.00 (summer); 10.00–18.00 Tues–Sat, closed Sun & Mon, (winter). Admission charge

Rüütli tänav (Knight Street)
Historic downtown Pärnu is defined by its main pedestrian thoroughfare, Rüütli tänav (Knight Street). The 400 m (440 yds) stretch of the street between Ringi and Vee, and a few streets that branch off from here, are home to a hodge-podge of intriguing buildings dating from the 17th to the 20th centuries. This is also where you'll find Pärnu's most exclusive shops.

CULTURE

Agape Centre/Agape United Methodist Church
The church has an active congregation and a lively cultural centre, with frequent performances in summer. ⓐ Männi 2a ☎ 445 9888 Ⓦ www.agapekeskus.ee ⌚ 10.00–14.00 Mon–Thur, closed Fri–Sun

Chaplin Centre (Museum of New Art)
Named after Charlie Chaplin, this cultural centre is housed in a former Communist Party HQ. ⓐ Esplanaadi 10 ☎ 443 0772 Ⓦ www.chaplin.ee ⌚ 09.00–21.00

THE ESTONIAN PLAYGROUND
Pärnu is where Estonians, especially from Tallinn, come to play and relax during the long days of summer. If you fancy joining them check out the opportunities below:

Bowling
Tervise Paradiis Spa Hotel & Water Park This large recreation complex was opened in 2004 and includes not just bowling but a host of other amenities, including a two-storey water park.
ⓐ Side 14 ❶ 445 1600 Ⓦ www.terviseparadiis.ee ⏱ 12.00–24.00 Mon–Thur & Sun, 11.00–01.00 Fri & Sat

Canoe trips
Edela Loodusmatkad Gentle canoeing adventures, either on slow-moving rivers or on the rapids on River Pärnu.
ⓐ Pärnade pst. 11, Paikuse ❶ 505 1113 Ⓦ www.loodusmatkad.ee
Fluvius kanuumatkad A chance to explore and view the scenery from the water. Ⓦ www.kanuuretked.ee

Golf
Golf is relatively new to Estonia, but demand has produced a host of good courses. Two of the best are:
Estonian Golf & Country Club This brand new course is called a country club but is also open to the public. It has two courses, the newest Stone Course and the slightly older Sea Course, which has grand fairways running along the sea.
ⓐ Manniva near Jõelähtme ❶ 649 8201 Ⓦ www.egcc.ee

Tallinn Golf Club Also known as Niitvälja, Estonia's oldest golf course is a favourite for many, given its proximity to Tallinn. Less challenging than Estonian Golf & Country Club. ⓐ Keila parish ⓣ 678 0454 ⓦ www.egk-golf.ee

Two of the less-challenging courses are:
Audru Golf ⓐ Audru Golf, Jõõpre, Audru vald ⓣ 505 9868 ⓦ www.audrugolf.com
Valgeranna Golf ⓐ Villa Andropoff, Audru vald ⓣ 444 3453 ⓦ www.villaandropoff.fi

Hiking
Maria talu This farm has a camping area, with horse riding and organised hikes. ⓐ Kõpu küla, Tõstamaa vald ⓣ 447 4558/523 6066 ⓦ www.maria.ee
Tolli Tourism Farm Another farm, this one on Kinhu island, offering hiking and camping packages. ⓐ Sääre küla, Kihnu vald ⓣ 52 77 380 ⓦ www.kihnutalu.ee

Horse riding
Maria talu Farmstead offering horse riding and other outdoor activities. ⓐ Kõpu küla, Tõstamaa vald ⓣ 447 4558/523 6066 ⓦ www.maria.ee
Riisa rantso A touch of western style, for riding lessons and for horse trekking. ⓐ Riisa küla, Tori vald ⓣ 510 0832 ⓦ www.riisarantso.ee

◀ *The beach is always very busy at the height of summer*

Tori Stud Horse riding plus sightseeing trips in horse-drawn wagons at the stables where they breed the good-natured and elegant Tori horse. In winter, wagons are replaced by sledges to get you through the snow. ❸ Pärnu mnt. 12, Tori alevik, Tori vald ❶ 528 6284 Ⓦ www.torihobune.ee

Saunas
Pühamüristus ❸ Saarisoo, Jõesuu ❶ 506 1896
Ⓦ www.soomaa.com
Tori kanuumatkad ❸ Põrguwärk Tori ❶ 511 4253
Ⓦ www.tori.ee

Spas: see Spas outside Tallinn, page 136

Eliisabeti Church
This historic 18th-century church, with its lovely interior, is also one of Pärnu's favoured concert venues. ❸ Nikolai 22 ❶ 443 1381

Endla Theatre
This theatre is one of the town's major cultural centres, hosting all manner of events. There's also an on-site café and gallery.
❸ Keskväljak 1 ❶ 442 0667 Ⓦ www.endla.ee

Pärnu Concert Hall
Right next to the river, this concert venue, the biggest in Pärnu, hosts international names when they come to town. ❸ Aida 4
❶ 445 5810 Ⓦ www.concert.ee

Raekoda (Pärnu Town Hall)

The Town Hall stages concerts and other events throughout summer. It's a particularly lovely place to hear classical music.
ⓐ Suursepa 16 ⓣ 443 1325

Theatre Gallery

This building houses not only the town's largest drama theatre but also an art exhibition space. ⓐ Keskväljak 1 ⓣ 442 0667
ⓦ www.endla.ee ⓛ 11.00–17.00 Mon–Fri

RETAIL THERAPY

Rüütli Street For a touch more individualism in the town's main shopping area, wander this street.

Yasmina Shopping Centre The most central shopping centre, where you should find everything you forgot to bring on your holiday. ⓐ Aida 9

TAKING A BREAK

AS Pere £ Just next to the bus station, this bakery/café provides some of the freshest cookies and cakes available. ⓐ Ringi 3
ⓣ 443 0117 ⓦ www.pereleib.ee ⓛ 07.30–18.30 Mon-Fri, 07.30–16.00 Sat, 09.00–15.00 Sun

Chaplin Centre Café £ The café in the lobby of the art centre is a popular and cheap meeting place. ⓐ Esplanaadi 10 ⓣ 443 0772
ⓦ www.chaplin.ee ⓛ 09.00–21.00

Sõõrikubaar £ This café-bakery is particularly famous for its *sõõrikud* (Estonian doughnuts). ❸ Pühavaimu 15 ❶ 444 5334 ❶ 07.30–20.00 Mon–Sat, 09.00–17.00 Sun

Kadri £–££ A friendly, long-established restaurant serving traditional Estonian cuisine at low prices. ❸ Nikolai 12 ❶ 442 9782 ❶ 07.30–21.00 Mon–Fri, 09.00–21.00 Sat, 09.00–18.00 Sun

Mõnus Margarita ££ This restaurant has won all the Estonian awards for its pleasant atmosphere and service. The food is Mexican, but if you're accustomed to spicy food ask the chef to make it hot. ❸ Akadeemia 5 ❶ 443 0329 ❶ 11.00–01.00 Fri–Sun, 11.00–23.00 Mon–Thur ❶ www.servitris.ee/texmex.html

AFTER DARK

RESTAURANTS
Brasserie £ If you have a big appetite, bring it to the restaurant at the Strand Hotel. Both breakfast and dinner are buffet style. ❸ A H Tammsaare pst. 35 ❶ 447 5370 ❶ www.strand.ee

Kuursaal £–££ Estonia's biggest tavern, the historic, 1890s-era Kuursaal near the beach, is also a venue for events. A popular stop for beach-goers looking for just a snack or one of the 'big bellyful' meals. ❸ Mere pst. 22 ❶ 442 0367 ❶ www.kuur.ee ❶ 12.00–02.00 Mon–Thur & Sun, 12.00–04.00 Fri & Sat

Café Grand ££ When it opened its doors in 1927, the Café attracted the cream of the local society. It has live music on Friday and Saturday

● *Outdoor cafés are great places to relax and people-watch*

nights. ❷ Kuninga 25 ☎ 444 3412 ⓦ www.victoriahotel.ee
🕓 12.00–23.30 Mon–Fri, 12.00–22.00 Sat & Sun

Lahke Madjar ££ A friendly, relaxed place, the 'Generous Magyar'
offers mounds of hearty Hungarian dishes. ❷ Kuninga 18
☎ 444 0104 ⓦ www.servitris.ee 🕓 12.00–24.00

Seegi Maja ££–£££ The surroundings will make you think you
have stepped back into the 17th century. Feast on items that might
have graced the plate of Peter the Great (freshly made, of course).
❷ Hospidali 1 ☎ 443 0555 ⓦ www.seegimaja.ee

BAR
Kadunud Lootus This simple pub, whose name translates rather
poignantly to 'Lost Hope Pub', fills up quickly with locals. ❷ Tallinna
mnt. 12 ☎ 447 2119 🕓 12.00–24.00 Fri, 12.00–02.00 Sat–Thur

ACCOMMODATION

Konse Holiday Village £ A combination of a guesthouse and caravan park, Konse is a winner. Rooms are basic but clean, and showers/WCs are shared. There are 50 caravan slots, plus all the necessary facilities. Bikes, boats and jet-skis can also be hired. ⓐ Suur-Jõe 44a ⓣ 53 435 092 ⓦ www.konse.ee

Best Western Hotel Pärnu ££ A comfortable hotel close to the beach. Many rooms have lovely views over the town. Rates include breakfast and use of the sauna. ⓐ Rüütli 44 ⓣ 447 8911 ⓦ www.pergohotels.ee

Carolina ££ Opened in 2006, this is in a new building near the yacht harbour. Rooms are large and well equipped. ⓐ Ringi 54b ⓣ 442 0440/555 80225 ⓦ www.carolina.ee

Delfine ££ On the street that leads to the beach, Delfine offers stylish rooms and suites, with facilities such as Wi-Fi. Massages and facials are offered in the beauty salon, and the restaurant is highly regarded. ⓐ Supeluse 22 ⓣ 442 6900 ⓦ www.delfine.ee

Freven Villa ££ This is a historic residence of Pärnu with a tiny reception desk around the back. Rooms have their own toilets and there's a generous back garden for guests' use. Wi-Fi and bicycle rental, too. ⓐ Kooli 31 ⓣ 444 1540 or 566 86545 ⓦ www.freven.ee

Green Villa ££ It's hard to miss the bright green exterior of this restored 1930s villa. The historic interior is attractive, with fireplaces and original hardwood floors. The guest rooms are comfy. ⓔ Vee 21 ⓣ 443 6040 ⓦ www.greenvilla.ee

Hommiku Hostel ££ More like a small hotel than a hostel, Hommiku has singles, doubles and rooms for three or four people. All have their own shower/WC, TV and kitchenette (except the singles), plus internet access. The Old Town location is a further draw. ⓔ Hommiku 17 ⓣ 445 1122 ⓦ www.hommikuhostel.ee

Jahisadama Guesthouse ££ Right on the banks of the river, this has 18 brightly decorated rooms, each with its own shower and toilet. Staff can arrange extras such as boat rental and sauna sessions. ⓔ Lootsi 6 ⓣ 447 1740 ⓦ www.jahisadam.ee

Kanali Villa ££ This low-key, family-run hotel is in a quiet residential neighbourhood. All rooms have a shower and WC, while suites come with their own small kitchen. ⓔ Kanali 8f ⓣ 442 5846 ⓦ www.kanali.ee

Koidulapark Hotel ££ This building, dating from 1905, has been lovingly restored and turned into a 39-room hotel. Most of the features are new, but the feel is traditional. Wonderful views over the nearby park. ⓔ Kuninga 38 ⓣ 447 7030 ⓦ www.koidulaparkhotell.ee ⓛ Open Apr–Oct only

Promenaadi ££ A beautiful, painted wooden villa, built in 1905, on a quiet, leafy avenue. The brightly decorated rooms offer cable TV, fridge and their own shower/WC, and the location, close to both the city centre and Ranna Beach, is hard to beat. Breakfast not included. ⓔ Tammsaare pst.16 ⓣ 56 617 623 ⓦ www.promenaadi.net

Rähni Guesthouse ££ Each of the lovely rooms comes with a computer, printer, cable TV and fridge. There are also three apartments suitable for families. ⓐ Rähni 9 ☏ 443 6222 ⓦ www.delfine.ee

Sadama Villa ££ This villa dates back to the 1930s but was only recently converted into a hotel. It's close to both the city centre and the harbour area, with cheery bedrooms and a garden to relax in. ⓐ Sadama 13 ☏ 447 0008 ⓦ www.sadamavilla.ee

Villa Ene ££ This cosy guesthouse is just a few minutes' walk from the town centre. Rooms come with their own shower and toilet, satellite TV, fridge and coffee maker. Breakfast isn't provided. ⓐ Auli 10a ☏ 442 5532 ⓦ www.hot.ee/villaene

Alex Maja £££ Set in a little courtyard in the middle of downtown, this attractive hotel features decent-sized rooms with cheery décor. ⓐ Kuninga 20 ☏ 446 1866 ⓦ www.alexmaja.ee

Ammende Villa £££ One of the best choices in this category, this impressive art nouveau building, surrounded by gardens, dates from 1905. The antiques-filled rooms are luxurious (those in the Gardener's House are plainer), and the suites are worth the extra. Splurge on dinner in the fine-dining room, and enjoy classical music performances in the garden or the salon on Thursdays. ⓐ Mere pst. 7 ☏ 447 3888 ⓦ www.ammende.ee

Scandic Hotel Rannahotell £££ The Rannahotell dates from 1937, when the Pärnu Beach was a magnet for beachgoers from all over Europe. Architecturally, the hotel is the epitome of Estonian functionalism. The restaurant is worth a stop in any season,

⬤ *Restored to its 1930s glory, the Rannahotell looks shipshape*

though it's ideal in summertime, when the large terrace is open.
🅰 Ranna pst. 5 🕿 443 2950 🌐 www.scandic-hotels.ee

St Peterburg £££ If a hotel can be a monument to the era of Peter
the Great, then this is it. Everything is decorated as if it were from
Peter's time, and the hotel has a wine cellar that the Tsar himself
might have liked. 🅰 Hospidali 6 🕿 443 0555 🌐 www.seegimaja.ee

Victoria £££ The Victoria is a Pärnu institution. It's not only
an excellent hotel, it's also a great place to have a quiet meal.
Take tea in the parlour and feel like royalty. The Victoria hasn't
been able to completely duck progress – it has Wi-Fi throughout.
🅰 Kuninga 25 🕿 444 3412 🌐 www.victoriahotel.ee

Tartu

The first written records of Tartu date from 1030. Now the second-largest city in Estonia, it lies 185 km (116 miles) southeast of Tallinn. It is known as a vibrant university town with a rich cultural heritage. In addition to Tartu University, founded in 1632, there is the Estonian Agricultural Academy and the Tartu Defence College. The city is also known for its research institutions, which represent most fields of science. The Emajõgi river flows through Tartu, adding colour to the city.

⬇ *The Emajõgi river runs through Tartu*

GETTING THERE

Tartu can be reached by car from the capital by following Tartu maantee (Highway 2). Frequent, regular bus services run between the two cities, with a journey time of two and a half hours for the express services.

The Tourist Information Centre in Tartu is a full-service affair, providing travel tips on all of southern Estonia. Here, staff will arrange guides and book accommodation; there's also an internet terminal. ⓐ Raekoda ⓣ 744 2111 ⓦ www.visittartu.com ⓒ 09.00–18.00 Mon–Fri, 10.00–17.00 Sat, 10.00–15.00 Sun, mid-May–mid-Sept; 09.00–17.00 Mon–Fri, 10.00–15.00 Sat, closed Sun, mid-Sept–mid-May

> ## CITY OF GOOD THOUGHTS
> Tartu calls itself the 'City of Good Thoughts', which is interesting when you consider it has so frequently been burnt to the ground by advancing and retreating armies. Tartu is the home of Estonia's finest university and, as everyone knows, university students make a town special. Rather than rush from place to place in Tartu, it's best to simply wander and see what grabs your eye. If you're lucky enough to be there for more than a day, visit the Supilinn neighbourhood. What used to be a district of ramshackle wooden houses is being reborn into what could become one of the country's great neighbourhoods. You'll find plenty of good thoughts coming from that area of the city.

SIGHTS & ATTRACTIONS

19th-century Tartu Citizen's Home

Providing a fascinating glimpse of what Tartu life was like in the early 19th century, this re-created middle-class dwelling from the 1830s is decorated with Biedermeier furniture. Detailed explanations in English help set the tone. ⓐ Jaani 16 ⓣ 736 1545 ⓦ www.tartu.ee/linnamuuseum ⓛ 11.00–18.00 Wed–Sun, closed Mon & Tues. Admission charge

A. Le Coq Beer Museum

On the A. Le Coq brewery tour you get a glimpse of the mostly automated process by which the company cranks out 40 million litres (10.5 million gallons) of beer every year. Most of the tour is spent in the beer museum, set in the old malt-drying tower that was still in operation until 1997. The exhibition starts with the beer-making culture of the ancient Sumerians and moves on to show equipment used in this factory since it started up in 1879. And, yes, you do get a sample at the end. ⓐ Tähtvere 56/62 ⓣ 744 9711 ⓦ www.alecoq.ee ⓒ Tours 14.00 Thur, 10.00, 12.00 & 14.00 Sat. Admission charge

Cathedral ruins
The huge red-brick structure at the north-west tip of the hill is the remains of the 13th-century Dome Cathedral. It was heavily damaged during the Livonian War and finally destroyed by fire in 1624. Today, it houses the University History Museum (see page 126).

Church of St George the Conqueror
This pretty pink Russian Orthodox church was originally built in 1870, then reconsecrated in 1945 after post-war restoration. If possible, try to look inside at the elaborate icons. ⓐ Narva mnt. 103

Church of the Virgin Mary
Built in 1899, this is a wonderful example of late 19th-century, neo-historicist architecture. The vaulted interior with stained-glass windows is well worth a look. The altar painting *Virgin Mary with Jesus* dates from 1905. ⓐ Veski 1a ⓣ 742 2731 ⓒ 09.00–11.00, 17.00–20.00 Mon–Fri, 09.00–10.00, 18.00–19.00 Sat, 09.00–14.00 Sun

Geoloogiamuuseum (Geology Museum)
Although this museum does contain a nice collection of minerals in the corridor, most of the display is taken up by hundreds and

hundreds of fossils – mainly small marine animals, but also primates and a few mammoth bits from Siberia. ⓐ Vanemuise 46 ⓣ 737 5839 ⓦ www.ut.ee/BGGM ⓛ 10.00–16.00 Wed–Sun, closed Mon & Tues Admission charge

Inglisild (Angel's Bridge)
Want to make your dreams come true? Hold your breath as you go across it, and make a wish.

Jaani Kirik (St John's Church)
This 14th-century building is Tartu's oldest surviving church. It was wrecked in World War II and stood derelict for nearly half a century, before being renovated, reconsecrated and, in 2005, reopened to the public. Inside and outside the church are around 1,000 terracotta figures. ⓐ Jaani 5 ⓣ 744 2229

KGB Kongid (KGB Cells Museum)
The KGB Cells Museum is housed in Tartu's infamous 'Grey House', which was the regional KGB headquarters in the 1940s and 1950s. Apart from the lock-ups themselves, the museum has extensive exhibits here on deportations, life in the gulags and Estonian resistance movements. ⓐ Riia 15b (entrance from Pepleri) ⓣ 746 1717 ⓦ www.tartu.ee/linnamuuseum ⓛ 11.00–16.00 Tues–Sat, closed Sun & Mon. Admission charge

Kuradisild (Devil's Bridge)
Just past the Church of the Virgin Mary, the Devil's Bridge was built in 1913 to honour the 300th anniversary of Romanov rule in Russia.

● *Tartu's Leaning House stands in Town Hall Square*

Lahemaa National Park

This huge park, which has nothing to do with swings and roundabouts and everything to do with finding new ways to preserve natural beauty, has been open for over 35 years. At least 75 per cent of its area is made up of forest, which gives scientists ample opportunity to study and apply various systems of biodiversity. Visitors will be treated to beautiful, natural landscapes and intriguing bays and peninsulas.

Leaning House

Estonia's 'Leaning House' – or Barclay House as it's officially called – stands in Town Hall Square. Builders in the 1790s unwisely set part of its foundation on the old city wall and another part on wooden piles. The latter eventually sank, giving the house its discernable lean. Thankfully, it was saved from collapse by Polish engineers, who shored it up during the Soviet period.

Mänguasjamuuseum (Tartu Toy Museum)

This museum, popular with adults as well as their offspring, displays everything from antique paper pop-ups to electric train sets. ⓐ Lutsu 8 ❶ 736 1551 Ⓦ www.mm.ee ⏱ 11.00–18.00 Wed–Sun, closed Mon & Tues. Admission charge

Pauli Kirik (St Paul's Church)

This towering church, with its distinctively square copper spire, is unlike the city's other churches as it was built by Finnish architect Eliel Saarinen in 1917. Worth a visit for a glance at its bright, art nouveau interior. ⓐ Riia 27 ❶ 742 0258 Ⓦ www.eelk.ee/tartu.pauluse ⏱ 10.00–17.00 Mon–Fri, 10.00–14.00 Sat, 09.00–12.00 Sun

Peetri Kirik (St Peter's Church)

Fans of all forms of Gothic ecclesiastical architecture will be
fascinated by this structure whose primary point of interest
is a two-storey nave that's surrounded by ornate chandeliers.
The fact that this church regularly welcomes a couple of
thousand worshippers is testament to many Estonians'
strong religious faith. ⓐ Narva mnt. 104 ❶ 733 3261
🕐 10.00–14.00 Tues–Sat, closed Mon, Sun after service

Sacrificial Stone & Kissing Hill

The huge stone here marks just one of the several hundred
pagan sites in Estonia. It is thought to have had some relevance
to fertility. Kissing Hill – the place to which local newly-weds
are supposed to repair for some quality nuptial time after the
brouhaha of the ceremonials – continues that theme.

Tartu Aviation Museum

Some of the home-produced exhibits in this museum
are a fascinating reminder that, not so very long ago,
Estonians were part of a huge and sophisticated system
of thought whose ideology was so opposed to the West's
that they were armed to the teeth in case the two cultures
descended into war. In today's vastly different climate, visitors
may inspect the huge range of aeronautical items on display
here (and we're talking everything from models to fully
operational fighter jets) at their leisure, without resorting
to furtive hidden camera work. ⓐ Veskiorg 1, Lange
❶ 735 1164 ⓦ www.lennundusmuuseum.ee
🕐 10.00–18.00. Admission charge

Tartu Linnamuuseum (Tartu City Museum)

The best overview of Tartu's history can be found at the City Museum, housed in a beautiful, 18th-century mansion just across the river from Old Town. The collection isn't terribly extensive, but all the major periods are covered. Don't miss the computer-generated video that shows what medieval Tartu would have looked like.
ⓐ Narva 23 ❶ 746 1911 ⓦ www.tartu.ee/linnamuuseum
🕐 11.00–18.00 Tues–Sun, closed Mon. Admission charge

Tartu University Main Building

This grand neoclassical structure was built in 1809 for the reopening of Tartu University. Inside, the University Art Museum houses a collection of classical sculptures, as well as a mummy from the 2nd millennium BC. Unfortunately, most of the sculptures here are plaster copies, as the originals were taken to Russia during World War II.

At the museum you can get tickets to see the fabulously decorated Aula (Assembly Hall), and the building's most interesting feature, the Student Lock-up, where, in the 19th century, students were incarcerated for minor offences. Cartoons and graffiti still cover the walls. 🕐 11.00–17.00 Mon–Fri, closed Sat & Sun. Admission charge for Art Museum, Student Lock-up and Assembly Hall

Town Hall

The striking pink building looming over Town Hall Square is Tartu's Town Hall. Built in 1789 by the town's master builder, Johann Heinrich Bartholomäus Walter, it mixes early classicism

◑ *Tartu University's campus has endless charm*

with baroque and rococo, and is the third town hall to have stood
on this spot, after the first two were destroyed by fire. In its day,
the cellar and the ground floor on the left side housed a prison,
while the right side was a weigh house. Today, the building serves
as the city's administrative centre. The 18-bell carillon rings every
day at 12.00 and 18.00. ⓐ Raekoja plats ❶ 731 1101

University History Museum

Part of the Dome Cathedral is now a multi-storey museum
detailing the history of Tartu University from its founding in 1632
to the present day. Everything from old laboratory equipment to
student life is featured. The beautiful old library is well worth a look.
ⓐ Lossi 25 ❶ 737 5674 ⓦ www.ut.ee/REAM ❶ 11.00–17.00 Wed–Sun,
closed Mon & Tues. Admission charge

Zoology Museum

The University's zoology department keeps a vast collection of
stuffed animals – everything from mice to giraffes is on display.
If you're not squeamish, check out the 'rat king' – 13 rats who went
about their business with their tails knotted together. This rare
find was discovered on a farm in Võru county in early 2005.
ⓐ Vanemuise 46 ❶ 737 5833 ❶ 10.00–16.00 Wed–Sun,
closed Mon & Tues

CULTURE

Tartu Song Festival Arena

This arena (which looks like a huge clam shell) was built
specifically to house the many festivals that celebrate Estonians'
passionate love of song, which is intrinsic to their culture and

was even the catalyst for the 'Singing Revolution' (see page 21). If you do happen to be visiting when one is occurring, you'll be exhilarated by performances given, especially those of entrants to the students' competition. ⓐ Laulupeo 25 ⓣ 742 2108 ⓦ www.arena.ee

The Tartu Theatre Laboratory
As with all theatrical 'laboratories', 'spaces' and 'exchanges', you should steel yourself for experimentalism before you visit. ⓐ Lutsu 2 ⓣ 5349 9811

Theatre Vanemuine (Big House)
This was established in 1870, and may well be the country's oldest still-operative theatre. There are actually three stages here (the Big House is complemented by the Little House and the Port Theatre), and many varieties of performance take place. ⓐ Vanemuise 6 ⓣ 744 0165 ⓦ www.vanemuine.ee

Vanemuise Concert Hall
This is Tartu's leading entertainments venue, and thus stages some high-profile, high-quality events. ⓐ Vanemuise 6 ⓣ 737 7530 ⓦ www.concert.ee ⓑ Box office 09.00–17.00 Mon–Fri, and one hour before performances

RETAIL THERAPY

Antoniuse Courtyard
All the products of Estonia's folk and traditional crafts – whether they're things that adorn your table, your bed, your ankles or your earlobes – are for sale here; and you can observe craftspeople in action, too. ⓐ Lutsu 5 ⓦ www.antonius.ee

TAKING A BREAK

Bistroo £ This modest little eaterie on the square has more than a hint of the functional-and-Soviet about its décor, but overcome that and you'll enjoy the fare. 🜂 Raekoja plats 9

Kondiitriäri £ This café knows all about the international lure of the aroma of pastries baked freshly on the premises. Leave your calorie counter outside. 🜂 Rüütli 5 ☎ 740 0366
🜔 www.pereleib.ee

⬧ Choose a central location if you wish

Opera Pizza £ The clue to the fare on offer here is suggested in the name – this is very much the place to come if you want to plunge your fangs into an Estonian pizza. ⓐ Vanemuise 26 ① 742 0795

Pagari Pood £ Another outpost of cake heaven, this splendid and welcoming café also serves some of Tartu's most fabulous coffee. ⓐ Raekoja plats 2

Café Wilde £–££ Although this café serves mainly traditional Estonian dishes (and excellent they are, too), it takes its name partly from Oscar of that ilk and partly from a certain Eduard of the clan. The Wilde attracts a lot of expats, so is the place for a natter in the mother tongue. ⓐ Vallikraavi 4 ① 730 9764 ⓦ www.wilde.ee

Crepp £–££ Once again, the clue's in this Old Town favourite's name: Crepp celebrates the crêpe, alongside a host of other French dishes bang in the middle of Tartu. The ideal place to debut that beret you've never had the nerve to wear at home. ⓐ Rüütli 16 ① 742 2133 ⓦ www.crepp.ee

AFTER DARK

RESTAURANTS

Big Ben ££ This is Tartu's English-style eaterie, and, like such places right across the planet, it majors in fish and chips, bread and butter and sausages and mash. So, if you need a bit of home-comfort noshing, get yourself down to this friendly café with all haste.

🅐 Riia 4 ☎ 730 2662 🅦 www.bigbenpub.ee 🕐 07.00–24.00 Mon,
07.00–01.00 Tues–Sun

Suudlevad Tudengid (The Kissing Students) ££ A lovely name
for a lovely café, which boasts its own in-house pub. This tends
to be the meeting place for the denizens of Tartu's bridge-playing
community, so you'll be more than welcome if you fancy a game.
🅐 Raekoja plats 10 ☎ 730 1893 🅦 www.maksuamet.ee
🕐 11.00–01.00 Sun, 11.00–24.00 Mon, 11.00–24.00 Fri,
11.00–03.00 Sat

🔽 *It's not easy to miss this particular version of the lost island*

Atlantis £££ This is probably *the* restaurant to visit in Tartu right now. It's posh and it's precious, but it isn't pretentious, and you can sample Estonian specialities in style. ⓐ Narva mnt. 2 ⓘ 738 5495 ⓦ www.atlantis.ee ⓛ 12.00–24.00 Mon–Thur & Sun, 12.00–01.00 Fri & Sat

Barclay £££ The Barclay Hotel has the (some would say dubious) distinction of having been the Red Army's HQ in the 50 years preceding independence. The restaurant has moved seamlessly into the new way of doing things by relying on the sheer quality of its service and fare (modern Estonian). A place in which to

indulge yourself. 🚋 Ülikooli 8 ☎ 744 7100 🌐 www.barclay.ee
🕐 12.00–22.00 Sun–Thur, 12.00–24.00 Fri & Sat

Püssirohu Kelder £££ This restaurant contradicts those who
would deny that you can have a slap-up meal in a former
munitions dump. The chef is justly renowned for the miracles
he can perform with a salmon. 🚋 Lossi 28 ☎ 730 3555
🌐 www.pyss.ee 🕐 12.00–02.00 Mon–Thur, 12.00–03.00
Fri & Sat, 12.00–24.00 Sun

Werner £££ Just up the stairs of the café of the same name,
this is a classy establishment whose gentleman's club ambience
seems to repel and attract in equal measure. 🚋 Ülikooli 11
☎ 742 6377 🕐 11.00–23.00 Mon–Thu, 11.00–01.00 Fri & Sat,
11.00–21.00 Sun

CLUBS & BARS

DcPlace Notable mainly for its décor – mechanical spinning
legs dangle from the ceiling and occasionally spring into action –
this is a fantastic spot for relaxing in the company of a student crowd
who now can't actually remember the Soviet days. 🚋 Küüni 2
☎ 744 1438 🌐 www.dcplace.ee 🕐 11.00–24.00 Mon–Thur,
11.00–02.00 Fri & Sat, 12.00–23.00 Sun

Illegaard Jazz Club This club runs the jazz gamut, right back
to Dixieland. 🚋 Ülikooli 5 ☎ 509 7795 🌐 www.illegaard.ee
🕐 21.00–02.00 Mon–Sat, closed Sun

Krooks It's definitely heavy on the metal at this gathering place
for Tartu's born to be wild crowd. Denim rock is worshipped

without so much as a blush here, and you'll find a hearty welcome from the head-banging patrons. ⓐ Jakobi 34 ⓣ 744 1506 ⓞ 10.00–15.00 Sun–Tues, 10.00–16.00 Wed–Sat

Õlle Tare It's hearty slaps on the back, vats of lager downed in one and the jaunty sound of the oompah-pah band at this German-themed boozeria. Whether you've got the legs for lederhosen or not, you'll have a wild old time here. ⓐ Aleksandri 42 ⓣ 734 1766 ⓦ www.olletare.ee ⓞ 12.00–02.00 Mon–Thur, 12.00–03.00 Fri & Sat, 12.00–23.00 Sun

Shakespeare It was a generous move for the land of Madis Kõiv to name a club after the Bard. Beyond the resonance of the name, this is notable for the music-and-speech recitals that occur frequently here. ⓐ Vanemuise 6 ⓣ 744 0140 ⓦ www.shakespeare.ee ⓞ 10.00–24.00 Mon–Thur & Sun, 10.00–02.00 Fri & Sat

Ülikooli Kohvik This is a hangout of the self-consciously intellectual students, so don't be surprised if you take your cake and coffee to the accompaniment of an incomprehensible, high-volume academic debate. But the verbal parry and thrust is always good-natured, and so the atmosphere benefits. ⓐ Ülikooli 20 ⓣ 737 5402 ⓦ www.kohvik.ut.ee ⓞ 1st floor 07.30–19.00, 2nd floor 11.00–23.00

Who Doesn't Like Johnny Depp? Whatever your response to the question that gives this friendly little club that's known for indie music it's name, you're almost certain to like the place itself as it's welcoming, intimate and has cheap booze. ⓐ Kompanii 2 ⓣ 502 6076 ⓞ 22.00–03.00 Wed–Sat, 21.00–01.00 Sun–Tues

OUT OF TOWN

ACCOMMODATION

Hostel Pepleri (Tartu Student Village) £ This central hostel –
actually University halls of residence – has got the lot, from
an in-house juice bar to Wi-Fi connection for your laptop.
ⓐ Pepleri 14 ❶ 740 9955 Ⓦ www.kyla.ee

Starest £ The big selling point of this hostel is the satellite telly
on offer. That said, the rooms are particularly pretty and the beds
are comfy. ⓐ Mõisavahe 21 ❶ 740 0674 Ⓦ www.starest.ee

Tartu £ At last: somewhere you would recognise as having
a cheery hostel ambience. That's in no sense meant to be
derogatory, as all facilities here are perfectly adequate.
ⓐ Soola 3 ❶ 731 4300 Ⓦ www.tartuhotell.ee

Tartu Student Village Hostel £ What a find! This is at the Hilton
end of the student accommodation range, and all but the fussiest
of budget-conscious travellers should do perfectly well here.
ⓐ Narva mnt. 27 ❶ 740 9955 Ⓦ www.kyla.ee

Park ££ The atmosphere of this charismatic, 1940s-built hotel is
one of a sort of film-noir laconic wistfulness. Rooms are perfectly
comfortable and the staff are friendly. ⓐ Vallikraavi 23 ❶ 742 7000
Ⓦ www.parkhotell.ee

Uppsala Maja ££ Tartu has many quaint buildings, and this
250-year-old wooden construction is chief among them. Rooms
are perhaps a shade small, but each one is cosy and personable.

TARTU

Take some photos: your friends back home will be envious.
ⓐ Jaani 7 ❶ 736 1535 ⓦ www.uppsalamaja.ee

Vikerkaare ££ If you want extremely quiet and extremely safe,
you should consider this guesthouse, which is right in the middle
of an otherwise residential area. ⓐ Vikerkaare 40 ❶ 742 1190
ⓦ www.hot.ee/tdc

Draakon £££ If your mantra is location, location, location, then
this hotel triumphs because it's central, central, central. That's far
from all, though, and the bathrooms are of palatial proportions.
ⓐ Raekoja plats 2 ❶ 744 2045 ⓦ www.draakon.ee

London £££ This classy establishment offers modern facilities in an
historical part of town. Rooms are nicely decorated in a Finnish style,
and the London gets a particular thumbs-up for its disability-friendly
approach. ⓐ Rüütli 9 ❶ 730 5555 ⓦ www.londonhotel.ee

Old Hansa Hotell £££ Tartu's historic, Hanseatic credentials are
exploited with great taste here, and the resulting 'olde worlde'
atmosphere is beautifully complemented by the Emajõgi river,
which flows just behind the hotel. ⓐ Aleksandri 46 ❶ 737 1800
ⓦ www.hansahotell.ee

Pallas £££+ The London's posh sister is one of Tartu's ritzier hotels.
What makes it really stand out is its interior decoration, which is
heavily influenced by the intricate beauty of the Pallas school of art
(the most famous sometime-member of which was Gustav Klimt).
ⓐ Riia mnt. 4 ❶ 730 1200 ⓦ www.pallas.ee

Spas outside Tallinn

If you want to extend your city break and fancy a few days'
relaxation or the chance to try indulgent beauty treatments,
then why not head to a spa? Or you may think your health
would benefit from professional treatment, medicine that will
go down all the better when it also offers the chance to explore
a little more of Estonia and the benefits of sea air. Tallinn has
several spa hotels, but there are also a number of impressive
spas dotted around the country.

On offer are a range of programmes from pampering beauty
treatments and massages to more invasive procedures – so do
check these are appropriate with your own doctor before you
travel. The cost of your stay will depend on the treatments you
opt for – check the spa's website for details of its packages.

HAAPSALU

Fra Mare Spa The question is: is it worth trekking 100 km
(60 miles) from Tallinn to hit the Fra? Well, the apparently
miraculous powers of its mud are renowned, and it offers
such intriguing treatments as ear candling and the chocolate
and/or red grape body wrap (there are worst ways of being
mummified). The resort itself is absolutely beautiful and
clinically hygienic. It's your shout, but we say go. ❸ Ranna tee 2
❶ 472 4600 ❼ www.framare.ee

---

❿ *Choose from a variety of treatments in the spa towns around Tallinn*

ISLAND OF SAAREMAA

GO Spa Hotell 'GO' stands for Georg Ots, the famous Estonian crooner who was a massive hit in Russia. GO Spa is probably Estonia's most famous luxury spa and indeed may be the best. It offers the usual suspects (massage, body treatment, hydrotherapy, facials) but does it in a way which keeps customers coming back. Also, the spa cuisine is rather remarkable. ❸ Tori 2, Kuresaare, Saaremaa ❶ 455 0000 Ⓦ www.gospa.ee

PÄRNU

Estonia Spa This supersize complex seems to be forever expanding. Housed in three buildings, with the White House and the Green House connected by an elevated glass walkway, and the famous Pärnu Mudaravila, that beautiful, domed building near the beach. Each facility offers decent, hotel-style rooms and a full range of treatment options. Most guests arrive in large groups and convalesce here for a week, so it's best to book at least a month in advance. ❸ Tammsaare tee 4a ❶ 447 6905 Ⓦ www.spaestonia.ee

Sõprus Health Rehabilitation Centre Some guests prefer to stay in the spa's classic yellow wooden villa, but, most are housed in the more modern adjacent building attached to the treatment centre. Rooms are all fully fitted out – some have balconies, and most have internet connections. ❸ Eha 2, Pärnu ❶ 445 0750 Ⓦ www.spahotelsoprus.com

Tervise Paradiis The largest spa hotel in Estonia has seven buildings connected by glass galleries, which gives them a decidedly space-age

look. A full range of therapies is available and rooms here
rival those in Pärnu's best hotels. ❷ Side 14 ❶ 445 1606
Ⓦ www.terviseparadiis.ee

Viiking Hotel & Health Rehabilitation Centre This attractive,
modern sanatorium near the yacht harbour is also a fine hotel,
a few steps ahead of others in town in terms of comfort. Healthy
services run the whole gamut, from infra-red sauna to honey
massage. This is also one of Estonia's leading cardiac treatment
centres, so don't worry about over-exerting yourself during your
stay. ❷ Sadama 15 ❶ 443 1293 Ⓦ www.viiking.ee

Villa Medica Pärnu's smallest sanatorium is in fact a private
clinic specialising in the treatment of musculoskeletal problems,
but it makes its hotel rooms available to both patients and
non-patients alike. Day surgery, beauty treatments and
massage are also available. ❷ Tammsaare 39 ❶ 442 7121
Ⓦ www.villamedica.ee

EASTERN ESTONIA

Kalvi Manor On a first glance at this seaside manor house,
you might think you were in England, so sumptuous is the structure
and its gardens. It has every convenience the huntin', shootin' and
fishin' set could possibly demand. ❷ Near the village of Aseri, 100 km
(60 miles) east of Tallinn ❶ 339 5300 Ⓦ www.kalvi-hotel.com

Saka Cliff Hotel and Spa The neo-Renaissance Saka Manor and the park
surrounding it are situated on the limestone bank of northern Estonia,
where the 1,200 km (750 mile) Baltic Klint reaches its highest point.

Spa services include a range of massage treatments and both infrared and steam sauna. ❷ Kohtla vald, Ida-Virumaa, about 160 km (100 miles) from Tallinn along the St Petersburg road ❶ 3364900 ❿ www.saka.ee

Toila Sanatorium This sanatorium offers a comprehensive range of treatments, and is particularly strong on electrotherapy, massage and saunas. It has two features that may well be unique: a 'Salt Chamber', an area whose salty atmosphere is reckoned to help various types of chest problems and breathing difficulties; and a 21st-century version of a Roman spa ❷ Ranna 12, Toila ❶ 334 2900 ❿ www.toilasanatoorium.ee

MUHU ISLAND

Pädaste Manor This late-medieval manor has become the kind of pan-facility hotel in which lottery winners are advised to seek refuge while they work out what they're going to do with their winnings. Core health-improving treatments include aromatherapy, hay baths and scrubs, and auxiliary treats include a restaurant and cinema. ❷ Muhu Island ❶ 454 8800 ❿ www.padaste.ee

❿ *Tallinn is the gateway port to Estonia*

Directory

GETTING THERE

By air

The easiest way to get to Tallinn is by air. Tallinn International Airport is modern and user-friendly. It is serviced by direct flights with Estonia Air from 23 cities in Europe, including London (Gatwick), Manchester and Dublin. Easyjet flies to Tallinn from London Stansted. The airport has a full range of services, including currency exchange, banks and ATMs. It's wise to get some local currency before heading into town.

Tallinn International Airport ⓐ Lennujaama 2 ⓣ 605 8888
ⓦ www.tallinn-airport.ee ⓝ Bus: 2

Many people are aware that air travel emits CO_2, which contributes to climate change. You may be interested in the possibility of lessening the environmental impact of your flight through Climate Care, which offsets your CO_2 by funding environmental projects around the world. Visit ⓦ www.climatecare.org

By rail

There is a direct service to the Russian cities of Moscow and St Petersburg, and to the rest of Europe via Latvia. In general, railway systems throughout the Baltic States are poor. The *Thomas Cook European Rail Timetable* has up-to-date schedules for European international and national train services.

Thomas Cook European Rail Timetable ⓣ (UK) 01733 416477; (USA) 1 800 322 3834 ⓦ www.thomascookpublishing.com

By road

Driving across Europe to Tallinn can take a long time, with the total distance from Calais being about 2,460 km (1,540 miles). The roads are good and fast through Western Europe, but once you reach Poland the pace will slow, as there are few multi-lane highways in Poland and the Baltic States.

There is a regular bus service to Riga in Latvia and Vilnius, Lithuania, with connections to most other major European cities through **Eurolines** (Ⓦ www.eurolines.com) and **Ecolines** (Ⓦ www.ecolines.net), who run services to Tallinn from a number of cities in Germany and Eastern Europe. **Hansabuss** has recently added a new luxury bus service connecting Tallinn and Riga (Ⓦ www.hansabuss.ee/businessline). Aimed at coaxing business travellers out from behind the wheels of their cars, it is twice the price of Eurolines but the comfort and convenience are doubled as well. The bus offers free Wi-Fi for the five-hour journey.

By water

The Port of Tallinn is located about 1 km (0.6 miles) northeast of the city centre. There are regular ferry and catamaran connections from Helsinki, operated mainly by Tallink, Silja Line and Nordic Jet Line, and a ferry service from Stockholm run by Tallink.

Port of Tallinn ⓘ (+372) 631 8550 Ⓦ www.ts.ee

ENTRY FORMALITIES

A valid passport is required to enter the country. Since Estonia joined the EU in 2004, entry into the country for most people has become very easy. Entry from another EU country is normally quick, while entry from Russia can take some time. Citizens of most countries do not require a visa unless they plan to stay longer than 90 days. Children aged seven to 15 years must have their own passport when travelling to Estonia unless they are registered in a parent's passport, in which case there should be a photo of the child next to the name. Children under seven years do not require a photo if they are registered in a parent passport.

For more information or to check the visa status of your country, check the website of the Estonian Ministry of Foreign Affairs
ⓦ www.vm.ee/eng

🔽 *Ferries link Tallinn to Helsinki if you fancy heading to Finland*

There are some restrictions on the import of dairy products and milk. The import of tobacco products, alcohol and prescription medicines is allowed, but the amount is limited. Customs information for Estonia is available at Ⓦ www.emta.ee

MONEY

The national currency is the Estonian kroon (kr.). One kroon equals approximately 0.06 euros. The kroon is broken down into 100 sents. There are coins of 10, 20 and 50 sents, and of 1 and 5kr. There are banknotes of 2, 5, 10, 25, 50, 100 and 500kr.

Traveller's cheques can be exchanged in banks, but are less likely to be accepted in shops. Eurocheque is the most widely accepted traveller's cheque, but American Express and Thomas Cook are also accepted. Most larger hotels, stores and restaurants take Visa, MasterCard, Eurocard, Diner's Club and American Express. Many shops and restaurants, especially those frequented by tourists, will accept euros. However, it is always advisable to carry Estonian kroons with you.

Banks and ATMs are plentiful and easy to find in Tallinn. Banks are normally open 09.00–18.00 on weekdays, while some offices are also open on Saturday mornings. All banks offer currency exchange. Exchange offices are also found in larger hotels, the airport, train station, ferry terminal and major shopping centres.

HEALTH, SAFETY & CRIME

Estonia is relatively safe in terms of health problems. No immunisations or health certificates are required before visiting. If you plan to hike in wooded or boggy areas, you should be vaccinated against tick-borne encephalitis. The tap water is safe to drink, although it may be less than palatable.

Minor ailments can usually be treated at pharmacies, which carry a wide range of international drugs, from painkillers to antibiotics. Pharmacies are normally open from 10.00 to 19.00, but one, **Tõnismäe apteek** (❸ Tõnismäe 5 ❶ 644 3650), is open 24 hours a day. It is located near the city centre.

Major complaints are best treated at a hospital (*haigla*). Emergency treatment is free, but if you are admitted to hospital, you will be charged a fee for bed space and drugs.

The standard of medical care is high, and most doctors speak some English. There are private clinics with English-speaking doctors in Tallinn. EU healthcare privileges apply in Estonia, so travellers from the UK require a European Health Insurance Card (EHIC). However, this only guarantees emergency treatment, not all possible expenses, so you should have good health insurance when visiting Tallinn.

Estonia has a relatively low crime rate. However, tourist attractions, such as the Old Town, are prime hunting grounds for sneak thieves, muggers and pickpockets. Keep pricey mobile phones and camera equipment out of sight as much as possible, and leave expensive jewellery at home. If you have a car, park it in a guarded, well-lit car park. You should not walk the streets alone after dark.

If you are the victim of crime, be patient with the police. Many officers, especially the older ones, are not fluent in English. The police are generally courteous and businesslike, but can be slow in filling out crime report forms.

As a visitor, you are required to carry identification at all times, although it is unlikely that you will be required to produce it except when entering and leaving the country.

OPENING HOURS

Shops generally open 10.00–19.00 Mon–Fri, with early closing on Saturday. Some may open on Sundays in the main tourist areas.
Banks are open 09.00–18.00 Mon–Fri.
Museums' hours vary, with longer opening hours between May and September.

TOILETS

A triangle pointing down indicates the men's room (or an M or *Meeste*) and a triangle pointing upward is the women's room. The most central public toilets are to be found in the Old Town. Disabled facilities are available in Town Hall Square. The city also has several Swedish-built automatic WC facilities, which require two 1kr. coins.

CHILDREN

Tallinn, especially the Old Town, is a child-friendly place. As you walk the streets, daydreams of knights in shining armour and great battles fought to capture the castle are almost guaranteed, and with any luck you'll find knights, damsels and jesters wandering around, too. If you're after something more educational, head to **Epping Tower** (ⓐ Laboratooriumi 31 ⓣ 601 3001 ⓦ www.keskaeg.com ⓛ 11.00–19.00 Sat & Sun, closed Mon–Fri). Here you can try on chain mail, hold a medieval sword, learn candlemaking and hear stories from medieval experts about the ancient city. The Tallinn **Science & Technology Centre** (ⓐ Põhja pst. 29 ⓣ 715 2650, ⓛ 10.00–18.00 Mon–Fri, closed Sat & Sun. Admission charge, free with Tallinn Card), meanwhile, boasts oodles of interactive exhibits, computer classes and lightning demonstrations.

Locals also love to take their children to the zoo. **Tallinn Zoo**
(🅐 Paldiski mnt. 145 ☎ 694 3300 🅦 www.tallinnzoo.ee 🕐 09.00–19.00,
indoor exhibitions closed Mon, petting zoo closed Mon & Tues),
established in 1939, is home to over 5,000 animals representing
nearly 350 species. Kids will love the petting zoo filled with rabbits,
hamsters and other small, child-friendly animals.

For entertainment, try the **Estonian Puppet Theatre** (🅐 Lai 1
☎ 667 9555 🕐 10.00–18.00), which is suitable for children of all ages.

Children are also quite welcome at some of the more serious
places such as concert halls. However, it might be best to select
balcony seats in case you need to make a quick getaway at any
point. Most restaurants and cafés happily serve children, and some
even have a special menu. Estonians are so tolerant of children you
may discover the chef is willing to make something special to appease
a little appetite. When it comes to getting around, children under
the age of three ride for free on Tallinn's public transport system.
Need a taxi large enough to accommodate a pram or pushchair?
Advise the dispatcher and you'll be sent a car large enough to suit
your needs. Most department stores such as Stockmann and
Kaubamaja have nappy-changing facilities. First aid is available at
the **Tallinn Children's Hospital** 🅐 Tervise 28 ☎ 697 7113

COMMUNICATIONS
Internet
Tallinn is well served by internet cafés, which is not surprising given
the high level of use by its citizens. The cost is about 40–60kr. for
an hour. Internet access is also available in public libraries, but there
can be a waiting time to get on a terminal.

Tallinn is one of the world's first cities to offer free Wi-Fi access
on almost every corner – even garages have it. If you're travelling

with your laptop, visit 🔞 www.wifi.ee for the current list of hotspot locations. Many are free, and some offer access for a nominal charge. Plans are also being drawn up to offer free Wi-Fi on all public transport in Tallinn.

Public access to the internet is offered in the following locations:

@5 Tallinna ⓐ Kaubamaja Gonsiori 2

Apollo Raamatumaja ⓐ Viru 23

Balti Sepik ⓐ Süda 1

Café Espresso ⓐ Estonia pst. 7

Café Sookoll ⓐ Soo 42

Central Library ⓐ Estonia pst. 8

Central Post Office ⓐ Narva mnt. 1

🔽 *Signs in English make orientation in the city easier*

Demini Department Store ⓐ corner of Viru & Vene
Mustamäe Shopping Centre ⓐ Tammsaare tee 116
Stockmann Department Store ⓐ Liivalaia 53
WW Passaazh ⓐ Aia 3

For a small charge, internet access is readily available at the following cafés and locations:
Kaubamaja internet centre ⓐ Gonsiori 2, Tallinna Kaubamaja 5th floor ⓣ 667 3100 ⓒ 09.00–21.00
Reval Café ⓐ Aia 3 ⓣ 627 1229 ⓦ www.revalcafe.ee ⓒ 09.00–21.00

Phone

The telephone system in Estonia is reliable and easy to use. All numbers within the country have seven digits and there are no area codes. Tallinn has a good supply of public telephone boxes, but they use magnetic cards and not coins. The public phones offer international direct dialling and many have English-language instructions posted inside. If you will be making calls from pay phones, you can purchase cards in denominations of 50 and 100kr. These are available from

TELEPHONING ESTONIA
To call in, simply dial your country's international access code, then 372 (Estonia's country code) and then the seven-digit number. If you need to reach an operator, dial 16115.

TELEPHONING ABROAD
To call out dial 00, then the country code, as applicable:
UK: 44; USA & Canada: 1; Ireland: 353.

post offices, newspaper and tobacco kiosks, some supermarkets and the tourist information office.

If you have a GSM mobile phone, it is possible to avoid heavy roaming charges by purchasing a prepaid SIM card from one of the local services, such as EMT Simpel or Tele2 Smart. Starter packs and refills are available at newspaper kiosks.

Post

The Estonia postal system is very efficient. The Tallinn Central Post Office is conveniently located at Narva Maantee 1, near the city centre. There are also post offices around town. Many post offices have some staff who speak English.

The Central Post Office is open 07.30 to 20.00 weekdays, 09.00 to 18.00 Saturday, and 09.00 to 15.00 Sunday. Normal hours of operation for other post offices are 09.00 to 18.00 weekdays, and 9.00 to 15.00 Saturday.

The cost of sending a letter to the rest of Europe is 6.5kr., and to North America and Australia it is 8kr.

Besides normal postal services, post offices can also be used to send and receive faxes, and to use the internet.

Information on postal services is available at ☎ 661 6616 and at ⓦ www.post.ee

Faxes can be sent and received from several locations:

Hotel Radisson SAS Tallinn ⓐ Rävala pst. 3 ☎ 669 0000
Olümpia Hotel's Business Centre ⓐ Liivalaia 33 ☎ 631 5333
Tallinn Central Post Office ⓐ Narva mnt. 1 ☎ 625 7334

ELECTRICITY

The electrical system in Estonia is very reliable. It is 220 volts AC, 50 hertz. The plug is two pin, European style.

TRAVELLERS WITH DISABILITIES

The Baltic States have a long way to go to become truly wheelchair-accessible, or even wheelchair-friendly. Even in the larger cities, access to public transport and tourist attractions is lacking. The spa resorts have been catering to those with disabilities since the mid-19th century, and it is in these areas that you will find hotels and restaurants that are better acquainted with physically challenged travellers.

Tourist offices can be especially helpful in determining if there is suitable accommodation in the area you wish to visit if you make your request in advance. It's a good idea to double-check any information you receive, since some establishments will advertise services that are still to be implemented.

If you travel with a wheelchair, have it serviced before your departure and carry any essential parts you may need to do repairs. It is also a good idea to travel with any spares of special clothing or equipment that might be difficult to replace.

Associations dealing with your particular disability can be excellent sources of information on conditions and circumstances in other countries. The following contacts may be helpful:

United Kingdom & Ireland
DPTAC Ⓐ Zone 4/24, Great Minister House, 76 Marsham Street, London SW1P 4DR, UK Ⓣ 020 7944 8011 Ⓦ www.dptac.gov.uk
Irish Wheelchair Association Ⓐ Blackheath Drive, Clontarf, Dublin 3, Ireland Ⓣ 01/818 6400 Ⓦ www.iwa.ie

USA & Canada
Society for Accessible Travel & Hospitality (SATH) Ⓐ 347 5th Avenue, New York, NY 10016, USA Ⓣ 212/447-7284 Ⓦ www.sath.org
Access-Able Ⓦ www.access-able.com

Australia & New Zealand
National Disability Services Limited (formerly ACROD)
ⓐ Locked Bag 3002, Deakin West Act 2600, Australia
ⓣ 02/6283 3200 Ⓦ www.nds.org.au
Disabled Persons Assembly ⓐ 4/173–175 Victoria Street, Wellington,
New Zealand ⓣ 04/801 9100 Ⓦ www.dpa.org.nz

TOURIST INFORMATION
Estonian Tourist Board Ⓦ www.visitestonia.com
Pärnu Tourist Board Ⓦ www.parnu.ee
Tallinn City Tourist Office Ⓦ www.tourism.tallinn.ee
Tartu Tourist Office Ⓦ www.tartu.ee

BACKGROUND READING
Architecture and Art Movements in Tallinn by Sulev Maevali.
This readable, informative guide to the city's architectural
supermodels broadens out into a valuable cultural companion.
The Baltic States: The Years of Dependence 1940–1990 by Romuald
J Misiunas and Rein Taagepera. A study of the effects of occupation
that's all the more effective for its calm examination of some
horrifying facts.
Tallinn Through the Ages by Raimo Pullat. A charming, anecdotal
journey through the city's eventful life.

Emergencies

The following are all national toll-free emergency numbers:
Ambulance ☎ 112
Fire ☎ 112
Police ☎ 110

MEDICAL SERVICES
For entry into Estonia, it is advisable (but not mandatory)
to have a valid health insurance policy. No vaccinations or health
certificates are required. In case of accident or serious illness,
call ☎ 112

Pharmacies (*Apteek*) are usually open from 10.00–19.00,
but one stays open all night (☎ Tõnismäe apteek, Tõnismägi 5
☎ 6443650). Ordinary medication is available in all pharmacies.

POLICE
The Estonian police force (*politsei*) was established in 1991.
Officers wear dark blue uniforms, and have special uniforms
for festive occasions.

EMBASSIES & CONSULATES
Australian Consulate ☎ c/o Standard Ltd, Marja 9, Tallinn
☎ 650 9308
Canadian Embassy ☎ Toom-kooli 13, 10130 Tallinn ☎ 627 3311
Republic of Ireland Embassy ☎ Vene 2, 10123 Tallinn ☎ 681 1888
South Africa Representation ☎ Rahapajankatu 1 A 5 00160, Helsinki,
Finland ⓦ www.southafricanembassy.fi
UK Embassy ☎ Wismari 6, 10136 Tallinn ☎ 667 4700
USA Embassy ☎ Kentmanni 20, 15099 Tallinn ☎ 668 8100

◎ *Estonia's finest on patrol in the Old Town*

EMERGENCY PHRASES

Help!	Fire!	Stop!
Appi!	Põleb!	Stopp!
Ap-pi!	*Poleb!*	*Stop!*

Call an ambulance/a doctor/the police/the fire service!
Kutsuge kiirabi/arst/politsei/tuletõrje!
Kyut-su-keh keer-ah-bi/arst/po-lit-sey/tu-leh-tor-ye!

155

WHAT'S IN YOUR GUIDEBOOK?

Independent authors Impartial up-to-date information from our travel experts who meticulously source local knowledge.

Experience Thomas Cook's 165 years in the travel industry and guidebook publishing enriches every word with expertise you can trust.

Travel know-how Contributions by thousands of staff around the globe, each one living and breathing travel.

Editors Travel-publishing professionals, pulling everything together to craft a perfect blend of words, pictures, maps and design.

You, the traveller We deliver a practical, no-nonsense approach to information, geared to how you really use it.

Editorial/project management: Lisa Plumridge
Copy editor: Paul Hines
Layout/DTP: Alison Rayner
Proofreader: Wendy Janes

The publishers would like to thank the following individuals and organisations for supplying their copyright photographs for this book: A1 Pix, pages 17, 35, 42, 95, 101, 106, 111, 115, 121, 130–1, 144 & 155; Ann Carroll Burgess, pages 1, 25 & 82; Tom Burgess, pages 5 & 71; Scott Diel, pages 98, 99 & 124; Dreamstime.com (Allein, page 55; Pontus Edenberg, page 141; Taylor Jackson, page 33; Kutt Niinepuu, page 38); Tavi Grepp/Tallinn Tourism, pages 20, 23, 75 & 91; Kaido Haagen/Tallinn Tourism, pages 29 & 97; Imrek/Fotolia, page 41; iStockphoto.com (Adrian Beesley, page 65; Christian Champagne, page 19; emily2k, page 137; Tomaz Levstek, page 53; Marek Slusarczyk, page 60; Peeter Viisimaa, page 79; Laura Young, page 72); Meelis Lokk/ Tartu.ee, page 128; SXC.hu (Stefanie Leuker, pages 14–15; Enrico Corno, page 149); Mats Tooming/BigStockPhoto.com, pages 116–17; Toomas Volmer/Tallinn Tourism, pages 7, 9, 11, 44, 51, 67 & 89.

Send your thoughts to
books@thomascook.com

- Found a great bar, club, shop or must-see sight that we don't feature?
- Like to tip us off about any information that needs a little updating?
- Want to tell us what you love about this handy little guidebook and more importantly how we can make it even handier?

Then here's your chance to tell all! Send us ideas, discoveries and recommendations today and then look out for your valuable input in the next edition of this title.

Email the above address (stating the title) or write to: CitySpots Project Editor, Thomas Cook Publishing, PO Box 227, Coningsby Road, Peterborough PE3 8SB, UK.

3

COL

Make the m

BKB Verlag

COLOGNE AT A GLANCE

The Old Town

Cologne in the Evening

Cathedral

Romanesque Churches

Art Museums

3 Days in

Along the Rhine

Shopping and Strolling

Content

LEGEND

X Duration of the tour
◆ Opening times/
  departure times
▲ Transport stop
➤ see

© BKB Verlag
All rights reserved
Edition 2023

Editor:
Dr Brigitte Hintzen-Bohlen

Layout:
Andreas Ossig
BKB Verlag GmbH
www.bkb-kommunikation.de

German-English translation:
John Sykes

Printing:
Difo Druck GmbH, difo-druck.de

ISBN 978-3-96722-044-5

BKB Verlag GmbH
Auerstrasse 4
50733 Köln
Telephone 0221/9521460
Fax   0221/5626446
www.bkb-verlag.de
mail@bkb-verlag.de

This book is:

carbon neutral
and socially engaged
natureOffice.com | 2019-702-570215

Welcome to

... a city of a million people on
the Rhine, famous for art, Carnival
and Catholicism. It was the most
important place of trade in the
north of the Roman Empire, in the
Middle Ages a leading European city
thanks to holy relics and commercial
privileges, and today Cologne is Germany's fourth-largest city, a centre
for media and international trade
fairs, a business hub in the west, a
university city and a lively location
for art and culture.

More than 2,000 years of history
have made their mark on Cologne:
Romans, archbishops, merchants,
French and Prussian rulers have
all left their traces. Unique in the
world are the twelve Romanesque

Cologne ...

churches. The Old Town with its little lanes is picturesque, the cathedral a World Heritage site, and the museums are outstanding.

In addition to many sights, numerous events attract visitors from all over the world – whether they come for Carnival or Christopher Street Day, Lit.Cologne, the Comedy Festival, Gamescom, Art Cologne or the Christmas markets, they can experience the Rhinelanders' love of life all year round.

In contrast to other large cities, this "village" of a million residents on the Rhine has never lost its homely character. This has a lot to do with the many different quarters ("Veedel" in Cologne dialect), where locals feel at home, and with the mentality of the people, who say that "Cologne is a feeling" and feel warm at heart when they glimpse the two towers of the cathedral. The people of Cologne love their city, have a more relaxed attitude than residents of many other places, and don't always take things too seriously. This mix of light-heartedness and lethargy, tolerance and ignorance, big-city atmosphere and small-town idyll, cultural highlights and imperfections in urban planning make Cologne such a lovable place ...

About Cologne

● Cologne has its own "code of law", a wonderful description in the local dialect (called Kölsch) of the mentality here. The first two articles express a fatalistic attitude to life: "Et es wie et es" ("Things are as they are") and "Et kütt wie et kütt" ("What happens, happens") because, as the third article states "Et hätt noch emmer joot jejange" ("Things have always turned out well").

● The phenomenon known today as "networking", i.e. making contacts to cultivate mutual interests, is known as "Klüngeln" in Cologne, and the city has long worked on the principle of "you scratch my back, and I'll scratch yours". Those who went to the same school, or are members of the same sports club or Carnival association, naturally stick together.

● Cologne has become the leading media city in Germany. Five major TV channels, including the commercial RTL and the public WDR, as well as six radio channels, are broadcast from Cologne. A third of nationally screened TV productions, TV films, daily soaps, game shows and talk shows, including the leading talent show and "Who Wants to be a Millionaire?", are made in Cologne.

● Cologne University was founded in 1388 and is one of the oldest in Europe. It was, however, closed in 1798 under French occupation, and

did not open again until 1919 as the "new university in Cologne".

● As long ago as 1516 Cologne's brewers began to protect their local speciality, a light-coloured, top-fermented beer, by establishing rules and obeying the German laws on purity. They renewed this in 1986 by signing the Kölsch Convention, a voluntary agreement of the brewers of Cologne beer, called "Kölsch".

● Cologne-Bonn Airport has the only runway in Germany that is also an emergency landing site for the NASA space shuttle.

● From 1880 to 1894 Cologne Cathedral was the world's tallest building. At 157 metres it is the second-highest church in Europe.

● More than 60 years Europe's first suspended cable car has taken passengers 900 metres across the Rhine between the zoo and Rhein-

park, which was also opened for the Federal Garden Show in 1957.

● Cologne's prominent citizens are buried in the Melaten cemetery, which contains some 55,000 graves and is at the same time a nature reserve, home to many kinds of plants, squirrels, bats and more than 40 species of birds and insects.

● The Cologne biologist Bruno Kremer established that the Rhine is 1,230 kilometres long. Owing to a wrong transcription in the 1960s, its length is always given as 1,320 kilometres.

● Afri-Cola, a drink derived from "African cola bean", comes from Cologne and was registered as a trademark on 26 June 1931 by F. Blumhoffer Nachfolger GmbH in the district Cologne-Braunsfeld.

● On 23 June 1963 John F. Kennedy shouted the Carnival call "Kölle alaaf" in front of Cologne's city hall.

1. Heinzelmännchen Fountain
2. City hall
3. Archaeological zone
4. Duftmuseum
5. St. Alban
6. Gürzenich
7. Heumarkt
8. Alter Markt
9. Hänneschen Theatre
10. Tünnes and Schäl
11. Groß St. Martin
12. Fischmarkt
13. Museum Ludwig
   ► page 46
14. Wallraf-Richartz-Museum
   ► page 48
18. Ludwig im Museum
19. Café-Restaurant in the Wallraf-Richartz-Museum

W1. Früh am Dom
W2. Ex-Vertretung

D.-Ketzer- Straße
Bahnhofs-vorplatz
U Dom/Hbf S
K.-Adenauer-Ufer
Komödienstr.
Trankgasse
Am Domhof
Burgmauer
Hohenzollern-brücke
Unter Fettenhennen
Dom
Wallraf-platz
Roncalli-platz
Römisch-Germanisches Museum
Bischofsgartenstr.
W18
13
Hohe Straße
gasse
Am Hof
Gr. Neugasse
Rhein-garten
Sporer-
Str.
Minoritenstraße
Kl. Budeng.
Mühlengasse
Am Bollwerk
Frankenwerft
ALT-STADT
gasse
Bürgerstr.
Unter Goldschmied
Alter Markt
Unter Käster
11
Mauthgasse
W12
Salomonsg.
pforten-
2
8
10
Lintgasse
Mauthgasse
Brückenstraße
4
3
Alter Markt
Heumarkt
Salzgasse
Frankenwerft
Rheinufertunnel
Ludwigstraße
Hohe Straße
Mars-
Höhle
Marsplatz
Steinweg
Eisen-markt
A. d. Rothenberg
Buttermarkt
In der
14 W19
5
Heu-markt
7
9
Pegel Köln
Schilderg.
Martinstraße
Bolzengasse
Gürzenichstraße
Quatermarkt
6
Gürzenichstraße
Deutzer Brücke
Deutzer Brücke
Hohe Straße
Gr. Sandkaul
Kl. Sandkaul
Augustinerstraße
U Heu-markt
Leystapelwerft
Cäcilienstraße
Pipinstraße
Am Leystapel
St. Maria im Kapitol
Am Malzbüchel
N
150 m
Lichthof
Marien-platz
Königstraße
Rheingasse
An Lyskirchen

Day 1

A Walk Around the City

The Old Town

Cologne in the Evening

Cathedral

3 Days In

Romanesque Churches

Art Museums

Along the Rhine

Shopping and Strolling

A BUILDING SITE FOR 632 YEARS

It took more than six centuries to complete Cologne Cathedral. Around 70 years after the foundation stone was laid in 1248, the choir was consecrated,

but from then onwards construction work proceeded slowly and was officially halted in 1560 due to lack of money. For more than 300 years the massive torso with a builders' crane on the unfinished south tower was a landmark of the city. Work did not restart until 1842, now initiated by the Prussian authorities, and was completed on 15 October 1880.

COLOGNE CATHEDRAL – A WORLD HERITAGE SITE

How light is filtered through 11,263 coloured squares, why a shrine with holy relics has such precious decoration, and who are the patron saints of the city – find out in Cologne's most famous building.

These questions and many more can be answered by the ladies and gentlemen in red robes who carry wooden collection boxes. They are officially known as the cathedral *Swiss guard*, a reference to the pope's bodyguards, who traditionally come from Switzerland, and patiently answer every question. Their main duty is to maintain the proper atmosphere and good behaviour in the cathedral.

As if they were magnets, the two spires draw visitors to the cathedral, which rises like a dark giant between the rail tracks, busy roads and the overcrowded pedestrian zone. No other German city has an emblem like this. Planned to be the biggest cathedral in Europe, it is imposing for its huge dimensions alone: it covers an area of 8,000 square metres altogether, with a length of 144 metres and a width of 86 metres. The huge, colourful surfaces of window glass, a combined total of 10,000 square metres, are equally impressive.

It all began with an act of theft: after the conquest of Milan, in 1164

3½ TIP Before your trip to Cologne, book a *tour above the roofs* of the city to see the elegant iron framework above the cathedral vaults, enjoy spectacular views and explore little-known tower chambers holding the stores and workshops of the cathedral builders. (*www.domfuehrungen-koeln.de*)

the bones of the Three Magi were brought to Cologne as spoils of war, making the city one of the most important places of pilgrimage in the Christian world.

On 15 August 1248 the foundation stone was laid for a new cathedral

in the latest style of the age, French Gothic. It was to act as a gigantic shrine for the relics and to surpass all existing buildings.

In order to house the relics, the goldsmith Nicolas of Verdun made the precious *shrine of the Three Magi*, dating

from 1190–1220. It now stands behind the altar in the choir and is the main attraction inside the cathedral. Shaped like a basilica church, this is the largest reliquary shrine in the West. Its iconographic programme ranges from the Creation to the Last Judgement. The figures are fashioned from gilded copper, the front end of pure gold, complemented by filigree work in precious and semi-precious stones, including ancient gems and cameos.

The cathedral is also home to a host of important works of art. Among the most notable are the Gero Crucifix (made around the year 980), the oldest surviving monumental figure of the crucified Christ, and the *Altar of the City Patron Saints* by Stefan Lochner.

CATHEDRAL BUILDERS

Cologne Cathedral was completed in 1880, but the building work has never stopped. Scaffolding can always be seen on the church, because preserving it is a job that never ends. The artisans of the cathedral office of works continue

a tradition of craftsmanship that has survived from the Middle Ages. Stonemasons and sculptors are responsible for renewing the weathered stonework. They are joined by roofers, scaffolders, carpenters, painters, electricians and metalworkers. Glass restorers, glass painters and glaziers take care of the conservation and restoration of the historic stained-glass windows. A goldsmith and a silversmith have the task of maintaining the works of precious metal in the treasury.

www.dombau-koeln.de

(around 1442), a masterpiece of the late Gothic Cologne school of painting in the Lady Chapel. A 21st-century work is the *window by the artist Gerhard Richter* in the south transept. Consisting of 11,263 squares of glass in 72 different shades of colour, when the sun shines it generates a symphony of light.

One sight should on no account be missed: to get a wonderful view of the city, climb the 533 steps of the south tower to the lookout deck at a height of 97 metres. On the way up you pass St Peter's bell, affectionately known to the people of Cologne as *Big Peter*, at 24 tonnes the biggest free-swinging church bell in the world.

Domkloster 4 ▲ Dom/Hbf.
◆ *Cathedral: Mon-Sat 10am-5pm, Sun 1-4pm*
◆ *Treasury (Schatzkammer): 10am-6pm*
◆ *Tower: 9am-4pm (Nov-Feb),*
9am-5pm (March, April, Oct),
9am-6pm (May-Sept)

www.domfuehrungen-koeln.de
www.koelner-dom.de
www.koelner-dommusik.de

Have a Break

Some time in a brewery pub (Brauhaus) is an essential part of a trip to Cologne. Enjoy a glass of Kölsch beer and the favourite snack, halve Hahn, (➤ p. 56) in **Früh am Dom**. *Am Hof 12-18*
◆ *Mon-Fri 11am-midnight, Sat-Sun 10am-midnight, www.frueh-am-dom.de*

The Old Town

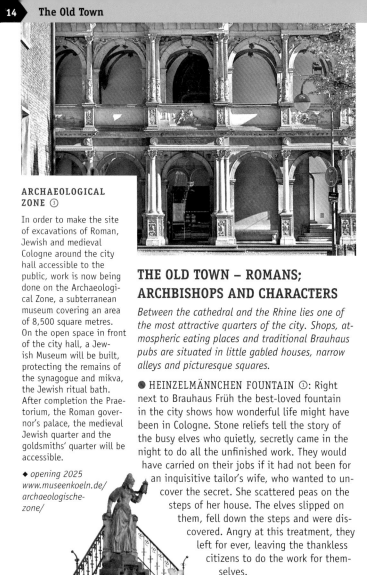

ARCHAEOLOGICAL ZONE ①

In order to make the site of excavations of Roman, Jewish and medieval Cologne around the city hall accessible to the public, work is now being done on the Archaeological Zone, a subterranean museum covering an area of 8,500 square metres. On the open space in front of the city hall, a Jewish Museum will be built, protecting the remains of the synagogue and mikva, the Jewish ritual bath. After completion the Praetorium, the Roman governor's palace, the medieval Jewish quarter and the goldsmiths' quarter will be accessible.

◆ opening 2025
www.museenkoeln.de/
archaeologische-
zone/

THE OLD TOWN – ROMANS; ARCHBISHOPS AND CHARACTERS

Between the cathedral and the Rhine lies one of the most attractive quarters of the city. Shops, atmospheric eating places and traditional Brauhaus pubs are situated in little gabled houses, narrow alleys and picturesque squares.

● HEINZELMÄNNCHEN FOUNTAIN ①: Right next to Brauhaus Früh the best-loved fountain in the city shows how wonderful life might have been in Cologne. Stone reliefs tell the story of the busy elves who quietly, secretly came in the night to do all the unfinished work. They would have carried on their jobs if it had not been for an inquisitive tailor's wife, who wanted to uncover the secret. She scattered peas on the steps of her house. The elves slipped on them, fell down the steps and were discovered. Angry at this treatment, they left for ever, leaving the thankless citizens to do the work for themselves.

● CITY HALL ②: 2,000 years of city history are concentrated around the Rathaus (city hall). The oldest testimonies to this are the Praetorium, seat of the Roman governor, and the remains of the medieval Jewish quarter.

The imposing *tower of the city hall* and its magnificent *Renaissance loggia* (1569–73) bear witness to the wealth and pride of the burghers in past times. As early as 1130 they had a "house of the citizens", which is thought to be the oldest city hall in Germany.

The tower was built by the guilds of craftsman between 1407 and 1414 to demonstrate their rule of the city. With its five storeys, it is 61 metres tall and is decorated with a sculptural programme showing 130 characters from Cologne history, and the *Platzjabbek*, the wooden face of a figure wearing a broad-brimmed hat and a beard beneath the clock. When the clock strikes the hour, he opens his mouth and sticks out his tongue.

The showpiece inside the city hall is the long chamber on the upper floor, adorned with fine stone tracery. It is called the *Hansa Chamber* in memory of the conference of cities of the Hanseatic League that was held here in 1367. Stone statues of the *Nine Heroes* on the south wall symbolise good government; opposite them on the north wall are eight figures of prophets (c. 1410) taken from a nearby room.

Rathausplatz 2
Visits only as part of a guided tour:
Tel. 0221/346430

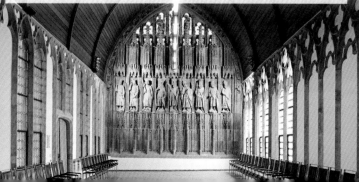

THE GENUINE EAU DE COLOGNE

The history of eau de Cologne goes back over 300 years, before the time of the most famous brand, 4711. Johann Maria Farina created a fragrance called Farina Original Eau de Cologne and supplied it to royal courts and

rulers in the 18th century. His success was soon imitated: in 1803 Wilhelm Mülhens acquired rights to the name of a Mr Farina, who was not related to the perfumer, in order to advertise his own perfume as a Farina product, and even sold on the name rights to others. 80 years passed before the Farina family could register their name as the first-ever trademark in Germany. Then the Mülhens family renamed their perfume after their house number (➤ p. 34).

● PERFUME MUSEUM IN THE FARINA HOUSE ④: On the opposite corner of the city hall square stands the house where the story of eau de Cologne began. In his small perfumery opposite a little square, Gülichplatz, in 1709 the Italian Johann Maria Farina invented a fragrance that reminded him of an Italian spring morning after rain, with the scents of orange, lemon, grapefruit, bergamot and citron, the blossoms and herbs of his homeland. The perfume quickly became a sought-after product in the world of the rich and beautiful, who preferred using perfume to washing, a common practice in the Rococo era. To find out more about eau de Cologne and three centuries of perfume and social history, visit the perfume museum (Duftmuseum).

Obenmarspforten 21
◆ Mon-Sat 10am-6pm, visits only
as part of a guided tour:
Tel. 0221/3998994
www.farina.org

● ST. ALBAN ⑤: Right next to the Wallraf-Richartz-Museum are the ruins of St Alban's Church, today a place of memorial for the dead of the two world wars. In the bombed-out church stands a copy of Käthe Kollwitz's work *Grieving Parents* (1931), bearing the facial features of the artist and her husband in memory of their son, who fell in the First World War.

Quatermarkt 4

● GÜRZENICH ⑥: A little further on stands a major Gothic secular building. Constructed by the citizens of Cologne in the 15th century on land belonging to the patrician Gürzenich family, it served as a venue for celebrations and a storehouse. Today the Gürzenich is the city's best-known place for congresses and events. To reach the great hall on the first floor, once the scene of receptions for emperors and glittering festivities, visitors pass through the spacious foyer and curving staircase in the extension built in the 1950s.

Martinstrasse 29–31
Visits only as part of a guided tour:
Tel. 0221/22123332

FOUNDERS OF THE CITY

Agrippa, who is portrayed on the ground floor of the Gürzenich, was a Roman general, a friend of Emperor Augustus. He was long thought to have founded Cologne, as he brought the Germanic Ubii tribe to the left bank of

the Rhine to be settled in the new town called Oppidum Ubiorum. In fact the credit for founding the city goes to Augustus, who order construction of an altar to the goddess Roma in 7 BC at which the Germanic tribes should pledge loyalty to the emperor each year, the basis for the community. The settlement gained its name Colonia Claudia Ara Agrippinensium (CCAA) in 50 AD, when Emperor Claudius, urged by his wife Agrippina, who was born there, granted municipal rights.

HÄNNESCHEN THEATRE ⑨

A shady courtyard is the home of the Hänneschen Theatre, a company with a long tradition that stages performances with puppets, a kind of commedia dell'arte in Kölsch, the Cologne dialect. The Hänneschen is a Cologne institution that has delighted children and adults since 1802 with puppets representing characters from the village of

Knollendorf. Usually the stories revolve around the everyday life of the main figures, Hänneschen and Bärbelchen. The characters Tünnes and Schäl are also involved, as is the fool of the ensemble, Speimanes, and the policeman Schnäutzerkowsky. All those who want to take a look behind the scenes can do so at the annual Hänneschen fair in May.

www.haenneschen.de

● HEUMARKT ⑦: Continue towards the Rhine to one of Cologne's largest squares. Heumarkt (Haymarket), an important place for trade in the Middle Ages, has been one of the leading open spaces of the city for centuries. It was once surrounded by the splendid gabled houses of merchants and artisans. As the approach to the bridge cut through it, it is now hard to imagine that this was once one of Europe's finest squares. The equestrian statue of King Friedrich Wilhelm III of Prussia, dating from 1878, surrounded by an illustrious circle of life-size figures including the Humboldt brothers, Friedrich Hegel, Ludwig van Beethoven, Karl Friedrich Schinkel and the art-collecting Boisserée brothers, commemorates the incorporation of the Rhineland into the state of Prussia.

● ALTER MARKT ⑧: A little further north lies Alter Markt, the commercial heart of medieval Cologne. The former appearance of this marketplace

can be seen by looking at the historic *Gaffelhaus* at Alter Markt no. 20/22. This Renaissance double building, the houses Zur Brezel and Zum Dorn, with their typical gables and fine windows, is one of the few imposing buildings that remain here.

The middle of the marketplace is occupied by the *Jan von Werth Fountain*, dedicated to a Cologne hero. Disappointed in love when he asked for the hand of the maid Griet, Jan von Werth hired as a soldier in the Thirty Years' War. Many years later, now a cavalry general, he entered his home town in triumph and, looking down from his horse, saw Griet, who had not married and was a poor market woman, selling apples by the city gate. When she recognised him, he said "Griet, if only you had married me!", at which she answered "Jan, if only I had known".

COLOGNE HUMOUR: THE KALLENDRESSER

Next to the Gaffelhaus, look up to see what Cologne people think of their rulers. Beneath the eaves there hangs a bronze figure called the Kallendresser ("one who shits in the gutter"), squatting and showing his naked backside to the city hall. According to a legend, the citizens were angry when the abbot of St Martin's handed over to the city authorities a criminal who had fled to the monastery hoping for sanctuary.

Alter Markt, the centre of the Old Town, is one of the pleasantest places in Cologne when the sun shines, and pubs, cafés and restaurants set up their tables and chairs outdoors.

RIGHT OF STAPLE

In the Middle Ages Cologne was a prosperous place of trade. The wealth of the city increased even more in 1259 when Archbishop Konrad von Hochstaden awarded it the Right of Staple, an important privilege. From that time all ships were obliged to take their wares ashore and offer them for sale for three days. This law corresponded to a geographical factor: as the Middle Rhine is shallower than the Lower Rhine, the goods had anyway to be loaded onto a different kind of ship in Cologne.

● TÜNNES AND SCHÄL ⑩: Pass along Brigittengässchen to see Tünnes and Schäl – the best-known legendary Cologne characters. Tünnes (the Kölsch version of Anton) is a harmless, good-humoured person, but his peasant cunning should not be underestimated. His broad potato nose has become shiny, as rubbing it is said to bring luck! Schäl (meaning "squinting" in Kölsch dialect, but also "bad" or "dishonest") is a crook. He is even more work-shy than Tünnes, has a big mouth, and is fond of drink and even a punch-up. He has a love-hate relationship with Tünnes: neither of them can get along without the other.

● GROSS ST. MARTIN ⑪: Here stands the Romanesque church St Martin the Great (1150–1240) that, along with the cathedral, dominates the Rhine panorama thanks to its central tower and richly decorated choir with the ground-plan of a clover leaf. This basilica is both the emblem and the name-giving church of the St Martin's quarter. Inside, the imposing architecture and plain furnishing come as a surprise. Don't fail to descend into the crypt, a journey back to Roman times. 2,000 years ago the site was an island, divided from the town by a channel of the Rhine, used first as a sports ground and later for building warehouses.

An Groß St. Martin
♦ Tue-Fri 9.30am-7.30pm,
Sat-Sun 10am-7.30pm
(August daily 2-6pm)
jerusalem.cef.fr/de/koeln-gross-sankt-martin

● FISCHMARKT ⑫: The Fishmarket, with a colourful row of narrow houses crowned by gables, is one of the most attractive spots in the Old Town. In the Middle Ages merchants

Have a break

Ex-Vertretung is a pleasant place for watching the comings and goings on the riverside promenade. *Frankenwerft 31–33,* *♦ from noon, www.ex-vertretung.de*

dominated the scene in the little alleys round about. The tower of the old fish warehouse is a reminder of this at the corner of Mauthgasse. Until the Right of Staple was abolished in 1831 it was used to store goods, and thus later got the name Stapelhaus.

FOLK MONUMENTS

In the Old Town local heroes and traditions are honoured. On Ostermannplatz a fountain refers to the songs of the Cologne singer Willi Ostermann (1876–1936). On Gülichplatz the bronze Fastnachtsbrunnen (1913) celebrates Carnival, and in the shadow of St Martin the Great a small open space called Rote-Funken-Plätzchen has a stone relief on the wall depicting a Carnival dancer (Funkenmariechen) with two members of a Carnival association and the text of the oath that they swear. An unusual monument is the square column (Schmitzsäule, 1969), 4.50 metres high, near Brigittengässchen, commemorating the "original" Rhinelander, whose typical name is Schmitz.

UGLY HEADS

In several places in the Old Town, grimacing stone heads can be seen on the walls (e.g. Salzgasse 2; Gasthaus zum St. Peter on Seidmacherinnengässchen). In the Middle Ages they had a practical purpose: instead of a lower jaw there was a hole in the wall into which a post was pushed. A rope thrown over the post was used to lower barrels or sacks into the cellar.

● STREET NAMES THAT TELL OF HISTORY:
On a walk through the Old Town you will see many unusual street names that tell of the history of this district. *Obenmarspforten* (Upper Mars Gate) refers to the time when the Roman harbour was built and the Mars Gate near this street was an entrance to the city from the river bank. *Judengasse* (Jews' Alley) and *Salomongasse* go back to the Middle Ages, when part of the Old Town was the Jewish quarter. The painters of signs (Schilder) lived in *Schildergasse*, the goldsmiths and silversmiths in the street *Unter Goldschmied*. Butter was bought and sold on *Buttermarkt*, fish was stored in the fish warehouse on *Fischmarkt*, and preserved in salt, for which the traders lived in *Salzgasse*. In *Lintgasse*, the basket makers used bast (Lint) to make ropes and baskets for fish. Around the corner in *Unter Käster* the barrels for most export salted Cologne's famous items, herring, were produced. The merchants sold their wares at stalls (Buden), which gave the streets *Kleine Budengasse* and *Grosse Budengasse* their names. Textiles were important items for Cologne's industry, as shown by the streets *Kämmergasse* (Combers' Alley), *Filzengraben* (Felt Moat) and *Rothgerberbach* (Red Tanners' Stream). Blue dye was made from the plant woad (Waid), which regional farmers sold in Cologne at *Waidmarkt* to the blue dyers, who lived and worked on *Blaubach*.

Lintgasse

Cologne in the Evening

The Old Town · Cathedral · Art Museums · Along the Rhine · **3 Days in** · Cologne in the Evening · Romanesque Churches · Shopping and Strolling

COLOGNE CARNIVAL

On the Thursday before Lent, when Fastelovend (Carnival) is opened on Alter Markt at 11.11 am, public life in Cologne comes to a stop. Everyone shouts "Kölle Alaaf" (Up with Cologne!), and revellers sing and dance everywhere, in the streets and in the pubs. The

top event is the parade on Carnival Monday (Rosenmontag). More than a million spectators line the route and hope to catch the sweets and flowers that are thrown from the floats. At the burning of Nubbel, a straw-stuffed doll, at midnight on the Tuesday, they say farewell to Carnival with tears in their eyes and yearn for the start of the new season on 11 November.

COLOGNE IN THE EVENING – FROM CLUBBING TO CLASSICAL OPERA

In Cologne there is so much to do in the evening that it is hard to choose. From theatre and concerts to a multicultural festival or a DJ night, in the Old Town or the Belgian Quarter, there are many options for entertainment!

● CULTURE: Cologne has a widely varied cultural life. In the Philharmonie, one of Europe's most beautiful and best concert halls, a high-class programme is staged. Concerts of ancient or modern music, including journeys to musical cultures around the world, can be heard at the *Musikhochschule* and the *Funkhaus* of broadcaster WDR. Cologne is known for its lively and innovative jazz scene: in the *Stadtgarten, Altes Pfandhaus, Loft, King Georg* and many other jazz venues, everything from classic big-band music to experimental jazz is on offer.

The *E-Werk, Wartesaal am Dom* and *MTC* are just a few of the locations where everything from Kölschrock to hiphop and house is played. And with the *LANXESS arena*, Cologne has the biggest indoor hall in Germany – not to forget the opera ensemble, which is performing in the Staatenhaus on the right bank of the Rhine until the refurbishment of the opera house has been completed. Cologne's theatre scene is equally diverse. In addition to the municipal companies, for example the Schauspiel playing on the Carlswerk site in the Mülheim district (➤ p. 61) and the *Hänneschen Theatre* (➤ p. 18), countless independent theatre ensembles enrich the cultural life of the city. Whether you like political satire or experimental drama, stand-up comedy or farce, there is something for every taste. To see listings of the programme of independent theatres, go to *www.theater.koeln*. If you prefer literature, take a look at the programme of the *Literaturhaus Köln*.

● GOING OUT: One of the best-known areas is the Altstadt (Old Town), where numerous pubs and clubs attract tourists and visitors from outside the city. The younger age groups go more often to the Ring, where they can party until the early hours at *Nachtflug, Diamonds Club, Das Ding* and *Vanity*.

BAP

"Verdamp lang her" (a hell of a long time ago) is the name of their best-known song, and it is indeed a long time since the band BAP was founded. In 1976 the singer and songwriter Wolfgang Niedecken, the "Bob Dylan of the Südstadt", started his Kölschrock band with other musicians. With role models like Bob Dylan, the Rolling Stones and Bruce Springsteen, today BAP is one of the most successful rock bands in the German-speaking world, now going for

40 years. Its membership has changed several times, but old songs such as "Kristallnaach", "Verdamp lang her" and "Aff un zo" still enthuse the public. BAP can fill Germany's biggest concert halls, but they have never lost their love of Cologne, and to all the songs expressing that love they have added their own: "Dausende vun Liebesleeder".

www.bap.de

The party continues in the **Friesenviertel** around Friesenstrasse in *Päffgen*, with Cologne's oldest in-house brewery, *Jameson's Irish Pub*, trendy places like *Heising & Adelmann* and *Päff*, and cult pubs such as *Klein-Köln*. Try *The Grid Bar* for cocktails, *Goldfinger* and *Flamingo Royal* for dancing.

Cologne's student quarter and probably its biggest party zone is the **Kwartier Latäng** (Latin Quarter) around Zülpicher Strasse. Old-established pubs like *Oma Kleinmann* and cult locations like *Stiefel*, the brew-pub *Hellers Brauhaus* and *Roonburg* are popular locations here.

The hip area is the **Belgisches Viertel** (Belgian Quarter, ▶ p. 36), where a host of small cafés, bars and restaurants have sprung up between designer shops and galleries. The heart of the scene is St Michael's Church on Brüsseler Platz, an open-air rendezvous in Cologne in summer. *Café Bauturm* and *Café Schmitz* on Aachener Strasse are Cologne institutions. *Ouzeria* and *Belgischer Hof* are just two of the attractive little restaurants around here.

Cologne people love their own Veedel (quarter).

One of the most popular is the **Südstadt**, with its concentration of pubs. The attraction here is the mix of authentic Cologne style of *Früh im Veedel*, long-established trendy joints like *Chlodwig Eck* and *Filos*, and newer clubs such as *Tsunami*.

Alternative subculture is found in **Ehrenfeld**, with a party scene in the *Live Music Hall*, the *Art Theater* and *Club Bahnhof Ehrenfeld*. The many pubs and bars include *Meer sehen*, *Hängende Gärten* and *Königsblut*.

There is plenty going on across the Rhine (▶ p. 44): dancing to techno in *Bootshaus*, one of the worldfamous clubs, in **Mülheim Harbour** and in *Elektroküche* at the Essigfabrik in Deutz. On the Rhine in **Deutz** there is no nicer place in good weather than *km 689 – Cologne Beach Club*. For traditional Kölsch style, go to the *Brauhaus ohne Namen* and *Lommerzheim*, a pub with cult status. For listings on where to go out in Cologne, see *koelnparty.de*.

Day 2

Romanesque Churches

3 Days In

The Old Town

Cathedral

Art Museums

Along the Rhine

Shopping and Strolling

Cologne in the Evening

Romanesque Churches

THE LEGEND OF ST URSULA

The legend says that Ursula, a Breton princess on a pilgrimage with ten girl companions and her bridegroom Aetherius, came from Rome to Cologne, where they fell into the hands of the Huns and were killed. At this a host of angels drove the heathen Huns from the gates of the city. In gratitude for their deliverance, the people of Cologne buried the holy virgins and dedicated a church to them. To this day the eleven flames in the city coat of arms refer to the martyrdom.

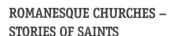

ROMANESQUE CHURCHES – STORIES OF SAINTS

In a city where there was once a church for every day of the year, including a collection of Romanesque churches unique in the world, a visit to at least one of them is a must. If that is not enough, there is the unusual museum of the archdiocese of Cologne, where modern and ancient religious art are shown side by side.

● ST URSULA ①: Have you ever been in a "chamber of horrors"? If not, don't fail to visit the church dedicated to Cologne's patron saint, Ursula. A Baroque tower roof with a golden crown shows the way to this Romanesque basilica, consecrated in 1135. On the galleries above the aisles were displayed bones that were thought to be holy relics from the martyrdom of St Ursula and her followers, discovered in the Middle Ages on the site of a Roman cemetery. As a huge number of bones were found, in popular belief the number of holy virgins was inflated from 11 to 11,000, attracting many pilgrims to the city.

Countless bones, artistically arranged to depict symbols and inscriptions, and over 100 reliquaries in gilded niches adorn the walls of the 17th-century Golden Chamber, generally known as the Schreckenskammer (chamber of horrors). This is only one part of the church's fine interior furnishings, which include 24 painted panels of the St Ursula cycle by Jan van Scheyven (1456) about the life of Cologne's patron saint.

Ursulaplatz 24 (Nordstadt)
Tel. 0221/7880750
▲ *Breslauer Platz*
◆ *Mon-Sat 10am-12 noon, 3-5pm, Sun 3-5pm*
www.gemeinden.erzbistum-koeln.de

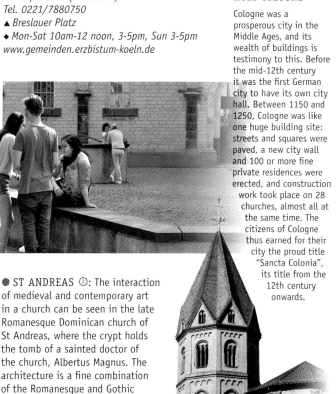

HOLY COLOGNE

Cologne was a prosperous city in the Middle Ages, and its wealth of buildings is testimony to this. Before the mid-12th century it was the first German city to have its own city hall. Between 1150 and 1250, Cologne was like one huge building site: streets and squares were paved, a new city wall and 100 or more fine private residences were erected, and construction work took place on 28 churches, almost all at the same time. The citizens of Cologne thus earned for their city the proud title "Sancta Colonia", its title from the 12th century onwards.

● ST ANDREAS ②: The interaction of medieval and contemporary art in a church can be seen in the late Romanesque Dominican church of St Andreas, where the crypt holds the tomb of a sainted doctor of the church, Albertus Magnus. The architecture is a fine combination of the Romanesque and Gothic styles, contrasting the opulent, ornamental sculptural elements of the Romanesque nave with the simple elegance of the late Gothic choir.

RELICS FEVER

No German city in the Middle Ages had as many magnificent churches as Cologne. One reason for the construction boom was the veneration of holy relics. As these

relics – the remains of saints – were thought to have supernatural powers and could work miracles, the churches were filled with more and more of these treasures, displayed in precious receptacles and golden shrines. The numbers of pilgrims who flocked to the relics led to the rebuilding of churches – for example in 1106, when the graves of Ursula and her followers were thought to have been found, and after the entrance of the bones of the Three Magi into the city in 1164.

No less impressive is the modern stained glass by the artist Marcus Lüpertz, which draws the eye like a "gateway to heaven". In the north transept, where Gothic murals depict scenes from the life of the Virgin Mary, the windows are devoted to the teachings of Albertus Magnus. In the south transept, known as the Maccabee choir because a golden shrine containing relics of the Maccabees decorated with episodes from the legend of the Maccabee brothers is placed there, the windows are also devoted to their martyrdom.

Komödienstrasse 6–8 (city centre)
Tel. 0221/160660
▲ *Dom/Hbf.*
◆ *Mon-Fri 8-11am, 1-6pm, Sat 10am-4.30pm, Sun 12.30-5.30pm*

● ST GEREON ③: The remarkable interior of a third Romanesque church, dedicated to St Gereon, is a good reason to add this one, too, to the list of visits. According to a medieval legend, Gereon was a Roman military officer who died for his Christian faith along with 318 legionary soldiers. When you enter the ten-sided building with its massive dome, slender pillars draw the gaze upwards. The glowing red of the dome with golden flames that refer to the Holy Spirit at Pentecost and the modern windows by

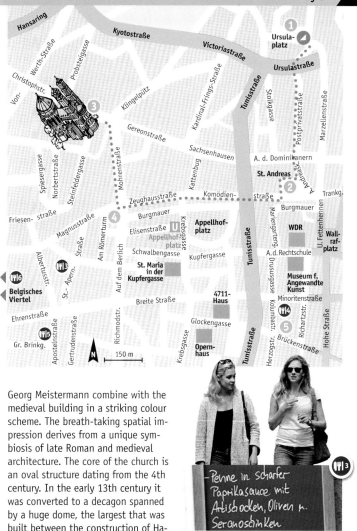

Georg Meistermann combine with the medieval building in a striking colour scheme. The breath-taking spatial impression derives from a unique symbiosis of late Roman and medieval architecture. The core of the church is an oval structure dating from the 4th century. In the early 13th century it was converted to a decagon spanned by a huge dome, the largest that was built between the construction of Hagia Sophia in Constantinople in the 6th century and the dome of Florence cathedral in the 15th century.

Gereonsdriesch 2–4
Tel. 0221/4745070
▲ *Christophstrasse*
◆ *10am-6pm*
www.stgereon.de

Have a break

After all this church architecture, take refreshments at the **Hase** restaurant with its Mediterranean cuisine and bistro atmosphere.
St.-Apern-Strasse 17
◆ *Mon-Sat 12 noon-4pm, 6pm-11pm*
www.hase-restaurant.de

● KOLUMBA (ART MUSEUM OF THE ARCHDIOCESE) ⑤:

The value of preserving memories and an example of responsible treatment of historic heritage is shown by the art museum of the archdiocese. The austere yet refined new building designed by the Swiss architect Peter Zumthor combines an archaeological excavation with the ruins of the late Gothic St Kolumba Church and the chapel Madonna in den Trümmern (Madonna of the Ruins) by Gottfried Böhm to form a harmonious trinity of place, collection and architecture.

ROMAN TOWER ④

That Roman architecture can survive the passage of time is shown by the north-western corner tower of the Roman city

wall, at the junction of St.-Apern-Strasse with Zeughausstrasse. Used in the Middle Ages as a latrine by the neighbouring convent of Poor Clares, and in the 19th century as the lower floor of a house, it is very well preserved. Mosaic patterns of various kinds of stone adorn the façade; the cornice and crenellations were added in around 1900.

Inside it is a lively museum with a "permanently moving inventory". Selected works from a remarkable collection that ranges from the early Christian period to contemporary art are presented according to changing themes, and visitors are invited to open up to unaccustomed sensory impressions. The museum team has long experience at creating contrasts between medieval saints' figures, madonnas and monstrances with works by August Macke, Andy Warhol or Joseph Beuys.

Kolumbastrasse 4,
Tel. 0221/9331930
▲ *Dom/Hbf.* ◆ *Wed-Mon 12 noon-5pm*
www.kolumba.de

Have a break

You have surely earned a stop to drink coffee. On your way is **Espresso Perfetto**.
Kolumbastrasse 8 ◆ *Mon-Sat 8am-7pm*
www.espressoperfetto.de

Shopping and Strolling

The Old Town

Cathedral

Art Museums

Cologne in the Evening

Romanesque Churches

Along the Rhine

3 Days In

Shopping and Strolling

COLOGNE'S BEST-KNOWN HOUSE NUMBER: 4711

Every hour, on the hour, a glockenspiel rings out on the neo-Gothic façade of a house in Glockengasse that has Cologne's best-known house number: 4711. This is the brand name of a famous eau de Cologne, and recalls the years of French

occupation. The French numbered all the buildings in the city consecutively, and the address of the Mülhens company (sold in 1994 to the Wella group) was given the number 4711.

STROLLING AND SHOPPING – AROUND NEUMARKT

For exclusive fashion around Mittelstrasse or hip shops in Ehrenstrasse, for branches of famous retail chains in Schildergasse and Hohe Strasse or young designers in the Belgian Quarter – in the centre of Cologne you can go on an endless shopping tour.

In the pedestrian zone along two main streets, *Schildergasse* and *Hohe Strasse*, which connect Neumarkt with the central station, fashion outlets and department stores as well as branches of inter-national chains present their wares for window shop-ping. Crowds of shoppers come here from morning to evening and all year round. An eye-catching building here is the Weltstadthaus by the star architect Renzo Piano. It has a resemblance to a glass whale, and is used by Peek & Cloppenburg to present an enormous clothing assortment on four floors *(Schildergasse 65–67)*.

Have a break

For breakfast or a snack, but ideally for its outstandingly fine patisserie goods, the café **Törtchen Törtchen** is seventh heaven for everyone with a sweet tooth.
Apostelnstrasse 19 ◆ 11am-6pm
www.toertchentoertchen.de

A well-loved attraction, not only for children, is the Lego Store on Hohe Strasse, where you can play with the coloured bricks to your heart's delight *(Hohe Strasse 68)*.

For exquisite and unusual items, or simply to do some window shopping, Mittelstrasse and Pfeilstrasse to the west of Neumarkt are an excellent destination. In the most expensive shopping street in Cologne and its side streets, exclusive fashion boutiques alternate with shops selling other extravagant goods. To cast your eye over international luxury labels, pass through the bright pink tunnel that leads to the Apropos Concept-Store *(Mittelstrasse 12)*.

Via *Apostelnstrasse*, where the old-established Filz Gnoss (felt goods; no. 21) is still in business, go on to Ehrenstrasse. Here stores for coveted labels have appeared between shops specialising in hip and in-your-face fashion. The esoterically inclined, shoe fetishists and lovers of kitsch will all find something to please. This street is a place to see and be seen, especially for a young crowd. If you prefer art and antiques, then nearby *St.-Apern-Strasse* around the Kreishausgalerie is the place to browse in galleries and antique shops.

KONRAD ADENAUER

On the north side of St. Aposteln Church stands a monument to Konrad Adenauer (1876–1967), mayor of Cologne and first chancellor of the Federal Republic. He was famous for his idiosyncratic ways of getting things done. While he was mayor (1917–33) the university was refounded, the trade fair grounds, Mülheim Bridge and Cologne-Bonn highway were built, the inner and outer green belts established and the Ford motor factory opened. "You achieve success in politics by being able to stay on your seat longer than the others," said Adenauer, a freeman of the city of Cologne.

3 TIP Twice a year, in the hip Belgian Quarter, the **Tour Belgique** opens almost every door and Brüsseler Platz turns into one huge catwalk and an open-air arena. The district devotes itself to culture, music, shopping and clubbing, shops stay open until 10pm and put on a special programme ranging from readings to concerts. Live music, live acts and other performances take

over the bars, while cool after-show parties are held in the clubs. Artists present their work and the quarter becomes a single, big open-air gallery (*www.le-tourbelgique.de*).

**THE RING –
ONCE THE PLACE
TO PROMENADE**

In the late 19th century the Ring, which forms a semi-circle around the city, was one of Cologne's most popular shopping streets. In the age of industrialisation the city was bursting at the seams, until in 1881 the medieval city walls were torn down and, following the example of Paris and Vienna, a broad boulevard with trees, fountains and monuments was laid out. Today only the renovated stretch on Kaiser-Wilhelm-Ring serves as a reminder of those days.

To leave the mainstream, go to the Belgisches Viertel (Belgian Quarter) around St Michael's Church. Young fashion and jewellery designers have set up shop in attractive old buildings. Visitors will find little-known brands, vinyl records, books, paper goods, gifts and much more.

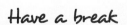

Have a break

With a view out onto Brüsseler Platz, stop at **Hallmackenreuther** to watch the goings-on and recover from shopping in a 1950s ambience.
Brüsseler Platz 9 ◆ Mon, Wed-Sun noon-6.30pm
www.hallmackenreuther.de

Along the Rhine

The Old Town

Cathedral

Cologne in the Evening

Art Museums

3
Days In

Romanesque Churches

Along the Rhine

Shopping and Strolling

HOHENZOLLERN BRIDGE

If you climb the cathedral tower, you can see that the Hohenzollernbrücke (1907–11) is in line with the axis of the cathedral. The previous bridge, the first permanent Rhine bridge in Cologne since Roman times, was built in the mid-19th century

with the same alignment. It was the wish of King Friedrich Wilhelm IV of Prussia that the railway bridge, as a symbol of technical progress, and the cathedral, an important medieval building and symbol of the German nation, should relate to one another.

ALONG THE RHINE – BRIDGES, BOATS AND A MUSEUM FULL OF CHOCOLATE

This walk starts from Heumarkt and passes Romanesque architecture and painting in Cologne's newest district, the redeveloped harbour called Rheinauhafen, and from there crosses the river.

● ST MARIA IM KAPITOL ①: From Heumarkt it is well worthwhile making a small detour to one of the oldest and largest Romanesque churches in Cologne (1065), which occupies the site of the Roman Capitoline temple. The magnificent combination of the nave with a "clover-leaf" choir, the first in the Rhineland, modelled on the Church of the Nativity in Bethlehem, was to point the way ahead for Romanesque architecture on the Rhine. Inside the church is a real gem: 11th-century carved wooden doors, with some traces of their original colours, that tell the story of the life and Passion of Christ. One curiosity inside is a so-called rib of the Virgin Mary, in fact a bone from the ribcage or jaws of a Greenland whale that had found its way into an arm of the Rhine in the Pleistocene era. Outside on Marienplatz is the Gate of the Three Kings, through which the relics of the Three Magi were brought on their procession into the city in 1164.

Marienplatz 19
◆ *9am-6pm*
www.maria-im-kapitol.de

● OVER-STOLZEN-HAUS ②: In Rheingasse stands a Romanesque house, the only one that remains of the impressive patrician family residences from that period. Today it is occupied by the Kunsthochschule für Medien (Academy of Media Arts). The opulent adornment of its five-bay façade with four storeys in its stepped gable, used for storage, testify to the wish of the Overstolz family to display the wealth they earned in the wine trade. They built the house in about 1220/30 as a place to live and do business.

Rheingasse 8, www.khm.de

● ST MARIA LYSKIRCHEN ③: On the way to the river you pass a small church that is closely associated with the Rhine. It was built in about 1210/20 right behind the city wall in a suburb populated by fishermen and river boatmen. Until 1868 the late Gothic "Boatmen's Madonna" that is now in the north aisle stood in a niche in the outer walls to bless passing boats. Inside the church, the colourful murals and ceiling paintings of the 13th century have survived the passage of time with little damage, and several restorations.

An Lyskirchen 12 ◆ 9am-6pm
www.lyskirchen.com

Rheinboulevard
KölnTriangle
➤ see plan in
front flap

UP AND DOWN THE RHINE BY BOAT

What would Cologne be without the Rhine (apart from having a cathedral)? The city is seen at its best from the river, and therefore a boat trip is an essential part of any visit to Cologne. For a brunch or a dinner with music and dancing, or simply for a cruise with a view, a round trip takes about an hour, passing the Old Town and going south to the old fishing village of Rodenkirchen or upriver past the Rhine cable car and the zoo to Mülheim and back. Trips start from several

piers between the bridges Hohenzollernbrücke and Deutzer Brücke:

KD Köln-Düsseldorfer Deutsche Rheinschifffahrt AG
Tel. 0221/2088318
www.k-d.com

Dampfschifffahrt Colonia
Tel. 0221/2574225
www.dampfschiffahrt-colonia.de

KölnTourist Personenschifffahrt am Dom GmbH
Tel. 0221/121600
www.koelntourist.net

● RHEINAUHAFEN: Cross a hydraulic swing-bridge next to the so-called Malakoff Tower, part of the Prussian city defences, to see the newest highlight of modern urban planning in Cologne, the Rheinauhafen harbour area. Built over 100 years ago for the trade in grain and wood, it has now become an attractive district for living, working and culture, with a fascinating juxtaposition of late 19th-century and modern architecture. On all sides you see the combination of historic materials such as stone paving, train rails and restored harbour cranes with huge slabs of concrete, steel and glass, set off by high-class lighting design. Despite the renewal of its appearance, the Rheinauhafen has not lost its original harbour character.

● CHOCOLATE MUSEUM ④: The eye-catching building beyond the swing-bridge, a glass palace that looks like the bows of a ship, was skilfully and harmoniously blended with the old customs offices. In 1993 Hans Imhoff, owner of the Stollwerck chocolate

factory, made his dream of a chocolate museum come true. On three levels, visitors can learn all about cocoa and chocolate, as well as about the history of the company.

Am Schokoladenmuseum 1a,
Tel. 0221/9318880
◆ *10am-6pm*
www.schokoladenmuseum.de

● GERMAN SPORTS AND OLYMPIC

MUSEUM ⑤: If you don't have a weakness for the sweet world of chocolate, walk a few steps further to the Deutsches Sport- und Olympiamuseum, housed in a protected monument, the old customs warehouse no. 10. On some 2,000 square metres of exhibition and event space it illuminates many different aspects of national, international and Olympic sports history, from ancient times to the present. The subject of trendy sports has its own room.

Im Zollhafen 1, Tel. 0221/336090
◆ *Tue-Sun 10am-5pm*
www.sportmuseum-koeln.de

3 TIP For a stunning bird's-eye view of Cologne, take a trip in the cable car that crosses the Rhine at a height of 50 metres.

▲ Zoo/Flora and Rheinpark
◆ 10am-6pm (Apr.-Oct.)
www.koelner-seilbahn.de

SEVERIN'S QUARTER

Between Chlodwigplatz and the bridge Severinsbrücke lies a quarter with an authentic, typically Cologne character, where natives of the city and newcomers, some of them foreigners, live side by side. Cologne people love this area for its Mediterranean atmosphere. In the narrow streets with little old houses there are many attractive shops, pubs, cafés and restaurants. Officially this district is Altstadt-Süd (Old Town South), but in dialect it is called the Vringsveedel. "Vrings" is the local version of the name of Bishop Severin. The church dedicated to this saint is one of the oldest in Cologne, and a landmark in the quarter.

Near the sports museum you can admire a well-planned combination of protected historic buildings with modern architecture: next to old warehouses on the peninsula between the harbour basin and Rhine, the three tall "crane buildings" ⑥ by Hadi Teherani are among the architectural highlights. The striking shape of these glass high-rises is a reminder of the cargo cranes of the old port. They are now a significant feature on the city skyline. Passing the *Rhine bastion* ⑦ and the *Kontorgebäude* ⑧, once an office building, walk on to an emblem of the city, a row of historic warehouses called the *Siebengebirge* (Seven Peaks) ⑨ because of their conspicuous gables. Now they house luxury apartments. Beyond them lies the modern *Kap am Südkai* ⑩, a ten-storey structure with a roof garden at the south end of the harbour development.

A major monument of the city is the *Bayenturm* ⑪, a fortified medieval tower – now seat of a feminist research foundation, the Frauen-MediaTurm – that was stormed in 1262 by the people of Cologne, protesting against the rule

of the archbishop. A popular saying has always maintained that whoever holds the tower holds power in the city. The next eye-catcher is the neo-Romanesque red-brick *harbour office* with its square clock tower, today the headquarters of the Cologne harbour and freight company, HGK.

Continue on the landward side of the leisure marina to *Kunsthaus Rhenania* ⑫. In this con-

verted warehouse, 50 artists from various countries work together on interdisciplinary projects. Unconventional architecture is on view at the *RheinauArtOffice* ⑬, occupied by Microsoft: two parallel façade strips link its separate parts and frame the transparent glass front. These self-supporting strips make intermediate walls unnecessary. Art is the theme once again in the *art'otel* ⑭ at the end of the marina, which is adorned with works by the young Korean artist SEO, a pupil of Georg Baselitz.

ART COLOGNE

For a week each year, Cologne becomes a focus of the international art market. For the Art Cologne trade fair in autumn, visitors from all around the world come to the displays of over 250 exhibiting galleries from Germany and abroad. It started in 1967 when a few gallery owners, including Hein Stünke and Rudolf Zwirner, founded the Kölner Kunstmarkt (Cologne Art Market) and showed contemporary work by little-known artists in the Gürzenich. The success of Art Cologne, as it has been called since 1984, was so huge that further art fairs have been established since then. ART + OBJECT takes also place in autumn. The focus is on Design, Antiques, Old Masterpieces and non-European art.

www.artcologne.de

Have a break
For mezedes and other Mediterranean delicacies, stop at **Limani** – the Greek word for harbour – in the Rheinkontor building. *Agrippinawerft 6*
◆ *Wed-Sat from 5pm, Sun from noon*
www.limanicologne.de

THE WRONG SIDE

Regarded by the Romans as barbarian, by archbishops as the land of heathen and by Mayor Adenauer as the first outpost of Siberia, the right bank of the Rhine has always had to bear prejudices. Its dialect name, "Schäl Sick", meaning literally "the squinty side", comes from the horses that pulled ships upstream and wore blinkers over their eyes to shield them from the sun. This made them squint, and they could not see the right bank of the river.

● RHEINBOULEVARD: Walk across the Deutzer Brücke to the other side of the Rhine, where the new Rhine boulevard including a flight of steps 500 metres long in front of the Hyatt Hotel is a good spot to linger a while. From here you have a superb panoramic view of the Old Town and the cathedral. It is one of the best places in Cologne to watch the sun go down.

● DEUTZ: For a long time the district of Deutz, which originated in a Roman fort, was overshadowed by the city quarters on the left bank of the Rhine. In the meantime Deutz has become a trendy quarter with a strong economic base thanks to the trade fair Koelnmesse, LANXESS arena, the TV company RTL, Lufthansa, Talanx/Gerling insurance, bee line and the Designpost. The most conspicuous landmark on the right bank is the innovative office high-rise called KölnTriangle. But this is also a good area to live, with a lot of pubs and restaurants. Thanks to the events at the Tanzbrunnen and in the LANXESS arena, Deutz buzzes with life, and both the Rhine promenade and Rhineside park are popular with walkers, joggers and tourists.

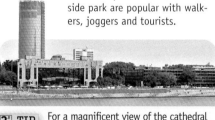

3 TIP For a magnificent view of the cathedral and surrounding area, take a lift 100 metres up to the viewing deck of the **KölnTriangle**. *Ottoplatz 1 ◆ Mon-Fri 12 noon-8pm, Sat-Sun 10am-8pm (Oct-Apr), noon-8pm (May-Sept) www.koelntriangle.de*

Art Museums

PATRONS OF ART

When the Museum Ludwig reopened in late 2001 with an exhibition entitled "Museum of Our Wishes", this was a celebration of a fine tradition of collecting and donating. Ever since the 19th century, citizens of Cologne have played an active part in shaping the municipal collections. When the French occupying government dissolved the monasteries and

religious foundations in 1802–03, Ferdinand Franz Wallraf and the Boisserée brothers bought works of art and libraries. The great patrons of the 20th century included Alexander Schnütgen, Josef Haubrich, Adele Rautenstrauch and Wilhelm Joest, Hans Imhoff and Peter and Irene Ludwig.

ART MUSEUMS – A PASSION FOR COLLECTING

Whether you would like to see the most important currents and viewpoints in modern art or follow the development of painting in Cologne between 1300 and 1550 – in this art city on the Rhine, both are possible.

● MUSEUM LUDWIG: Just as the museum catches the eye from outside with its stepped architectural landscape of brick-red walls and curved roofs, inside it holds an exceptional collection that delights art lovers. Since being re-arranged, the presentation is chronological, and will be in a state of constant change so that visitors can see, little by little, as broad a selection from the holdings as possible.

A circuit begins on the second floor with **modern works** that Josef Haubrich left to the city in his legacy of 1946. With works by Otto Dix,

Emil Nolde and Marc Chagall, Ernst Ludwig Kirchner's *Semi-Nude with a Hat* and Max Pechstein's *Fränzi on the Sofa*, paintings by Max Beckmann from the collection of Lilly von Schnitzler and much more, this is one of the leading collections of Expressionist art. The **Picasso collection**, the third-biggest in the world after those in Paris and Barcelona, is no less spectacular thanks to donations by Peter and Irene Ludwig. From *Harlequin* (1923) to *Woman with an Artichoke* (1941), all phases of the artist's work are represented, with paintings, ceramic works and sculptures. Russian avant-garde, Surrealist and Constructivist works round off the displays.

The exhibition on the first floor ranges from the abstract movement of the 1950s to the 1970s, including Action Painting, Minimal Art and Fluxus. Its highlight is the high-calibre **collection of Pop Art**, containing famous works such as Roy Lichtenstein's *Blonde M-Maybe – A Girl's Picture* (1965), Andy Warhol's *White Brillo Boxes* and Claes Oldenburg's *Soft Washstand*. Duane Hanson's famous *Woman with a Purse*, which puzzles visitors because it looks so real, is also here.

Have a break

After so much art you deserve a glass of Prosecco in the café **Ludwig im Museum!** *Heinrich-Böll-Platz (in the Museum Ludwig)*
◆ *Tue-Sat 10am-1am, Sun 10am-10pm*

The stairs to the lower floor lead straight to A. R. Penck's monumental painting *I in Germany (West)* (1984) and thus to **contemporary art**. Two installations, *Heaven's Book* by the Chinese artist Xu Bing and *Regatta* by the Cuban Kcho, represent Asian and Latin American works here for the first time.

It is certainly worth viewing the *Photographic Collection*, one of the most significant in the world. It includes early daguerreotypes, rare early works of photography from the 19th century, important artistic photographs, albums and extensive material on the cultural history of this medium.

Heinrich-Böll-Platz
Tel. 0221/22126165
▲ *Dom/Hbf.*
◆ *Tue-Sun 10am-6pm, first Thu in the month 10am-10pm*
www.museum-ludwig.de

● WALLRAF-RICHARTZ-MUSEUM & FONDATION CORBOUD: The Cologne architect Oswald M. Ungers designed the austerely cuboid structure that harmoniously blends with the historic buildings of the neighbourhood thanks to its simple geometrical form. Visitors are guided through various eras of art history on three floors and can see paintings made over seven centuries, from medieval beginnings until the early 20th century.

Two angels hold open a precious brocade curtain, revealing the Virgin Mary in paradise, surrounded by more angels making music. Stefan Lochner's painting for private meditation, *Madonna in the Rose Garden* (c. 1450) – also known as the "Kölsch Mona Lisa" – is just one of many masterpieces in the gallery with the world's most comprehensive **collection of medieval painting** on the first floor.

Jusepe de Ribera's *Paulus Eremita* (1647), Rembrandt's famous *Self-Portrait* (c. 1668) and François Boucher's *Girl in Repose* (1751) can be mentioned as examples of the Baroque art on the floor above. The art of the 17th and 18th centuries is represented through works by famous artists including Rubens, Bordone and Tintoretto, Murillo and Ribera.

A walk around the third floor takes the visitor from landscape painting of the early 19th century to the dawn of modern art. Impressionism is a strong point of the collection: with Auguste Renoir's *A Couple* (c. 1868), Vincent van Gogh's *Drawbridge* (1888) and Claude Monet's *Waterlilies* (1915/17), thanks to the collection of the Fondation Corboud art lovers can follow the course of Impressionism from its roots in Barbizon to the cube forms of Paul Cézanne and the Pointillist masterpieces of Paul Signac.

Tel. 0221/22121119
▲ *Dom/Hbf.*
◆ *Tue-Sun 10am-6pm, first and third Thu in the month 10am-10pm*
www.wallraf.museum

Have a break

Round off your visit to the museum with coffee and cake in the Wallraf-Richartz café-restaurant in the museum. *Café-Restaurant im Museum* ◆ *Tue-Sun 10am-6pm, first and third Thu 10am-10pm*

Accommodation, entertainment, tips and addresses

Hotels

FLORA AND BOTANICAL GARDEN

One of the oldest parks in the city is the Flora, next to the zoo. It was laid out in 1864 to plans by Peter Joseph Lenné, the landscape gardener of the royal park in Potsdam, and extended in 1914 by the addition of the Botanical Garden. Among its highlights are the first avenue of palms in Germany, the rose gardens and four connected hothouses,

which are being renovated at present. At the centre of the park with its mature trees, exotic plants, ponds, specialist garden areas and countless botanical species is the restored hall for festivities, newly built on the model of its 19th-century predecessor, including a café and a venue for events.

Im Botanischen Garten
▲ *Zoo/Flora*
◆ *8am until dusk*
Free admission

LOW BUDGET

● **CITY-HOSTEL PATHPOINT COLOGNE**
Allerheiligenstrasse 15 (city centre)
Tel. 0221/13056860
▲ Breslauerplatz
www.jugendherberge.de/ de-de/jugendherbergen/ koeln-pathpoint724/ portraet

Young backpackers from all over the world like this accommodation in a converted church close to Cologne Cathedral.

● **DIE WOHNGEMEIN-SCHAFT**
Richard-Wagner-Strasse 39 (Belgisches Viertel)
Tel 0221/98593090
▲ Rudolfplatz
www.die-wohngemein-schaft.net

The name says it all, here you feel like you're in a big cosy flat-sharing community.

● **HOSTEL KÖLN****
Marsilstein 29 (city centre)
Tel. 0221/9987760
▲ Rudolfplatz
hostel.ag

A modern hostel in a former office building in a quiet yet central location between Neumarkt and Rudolfplatz.

SUPERIOR

3 Days In ⎮ **TIP** ● **1ST FLOOR KÖLN**
Yorkstrasse 1 (Nippes)
Tel. 0221/99375904
▲ Florastrasse
1stfloorkoeln.com

Boardinghouse with comfortable rooms each individually designed in the fancy quarter Nippes.

● **CLASSIK HOTEL ANTONIUS******
Dagobertstrasse 32 (Nordstadt)
Tel. 0221/998000
▲ Ebertplatz
www.classik-hotel-collec-tion.com/hotels/classik-hotel-antonius

In what used to be a charitable institution caring for wandering journeymen, the charm of a historic building is combined with modern art and luxurious amenities.

● **HOTEL CHELSEA**
Jülicher Strasse 1 (Belgisches Viertel)
Tel. 0221/207150
▲ Rudolfplatz
www.hotel-chelsea.de

The Qvest Hotel

Hotel Excelsior Ernst

For over 30 years the Chelsea has provided accommodation for artists, who have left their mark here with their works. Other guests appreciate the individual style of the house.

● **HOTEL STADTPALAIS****
Deutz-Kalker Strasse 52 (Deutz)
Tel. 0221/880420
▲ Deutz Technische Hochschule
www.hotelstadtpalais.de

A first-class hotel in the former Kaiser Wilhelm Baths near the LANXESS arena and trade-fair grounds.

● **KONCEPT HOTEL INTERNATIONAL*****
Blaubach 13 (Old Town)
▲ Posttraße
www.koncepthotels.com/ hotel-international-koeln

A new concept of hotel business thanks to digitalisation between Vringsveedel and the old town.

● **STERN AM RATHAUS*****
Bürgerstrasse 6 (Old Town)
Tel. 0221/22251750
▲ Rathaus
www.stern-am-rathaus.de

An extremely pleasant hotel with a personal touch, only a short walk from the cathedral.

● **THE NEW YORKER HOTEL****
Deutz-Mülheimer Strasse 204 (Mülheim)
Tel. 0221/47330
▲ Grünstrasse
www.thenewyorkerhotel.de

A design hotel with sensual puristic rooms, very close to the trade-fair site and the LANXESS arena.

DE LUXE

● **HOTEL EXCELSIOR ERNST*****
Trankgasse 1–5/Domplatz (city centre)
Tel. 0221/2701
▲ Dom/Hbf.
www.excelsiorhotelernst.com/

A stylish grand hotel opposite the cathedral and close to the train station for guests who like exclusive surroundings.

● **HOTEL QVEST*****
Gereonskloster 12 (city centre)
Tel. 0221/2785780
▲ Christophstrasse/ Mediapark
www.qvest-hotel.com

An out-of-the-ordinary designer hotel in the former city archive, furnished with classic design items.

ZOOLOGICAL GARDEN

More than 10,000 animals from some 700 species live in the 20-hectare gardens of Cologne zoo, one of the most popular zoos in Germany. With its aquarium and insectarium, rainforest house, huge elephant park and hippodrome, as well as the latest attraction, the Clemenshof, a farmyard in the typical style of the Bergisches Land, it reflects both 160 years of zoological history and the transformation from a menagerie to a modern ark for protecting natural species. Its oldest monument is the former elephant house in Moorish style, dating from 1863.

Riehler Strasse 173
▲ Zoo/Flora
◆ Zoo: 9am-6pm (summer),
9am-5pm (winter)
Aquarium: 9am-6pm
www.koelnerzoo.de

Restaurants

COLOGNE IN NUMBERS

Cologne is one of four German cities with a population of over a million, making it the biggest on the Rhine. Around 212,000 Cologne residents, including over 53,000 Turks, do not have German nationality. 40 per cent of Cologne citizens are Roman Catholics.

The area of the city is 405 square kilometres, of which 230 square kilometres lie on the left bank and 175 on the right bank of the Rhine. The city boundary is 130 kilometres long. The highest point has an altitude of 118 metres, the lowest 37.5 metres above sea level.

Almost 140 square kilometres are built up; parks and green spaces account for 37 square kilometres; 82 square kilometres are devoted to agriculture; and the city has more than 56 square kilometres of woodland. In Cologne there are over 125,000 residential buildings. The tallest monument is the Colonius TV tower at 266 metres. It has been a city landmark since 1981.

The cathedral is the second-tallest building

● 485 GRAD
Bonner Straße 34
(Südstadt)
Tel. 0221/93293148
▲ Zülpicher Strasse
◆ Mon-Fri noon-3pm,
Mon-Sat 6-11 pm
www.485grad.de

A trendy restaurant that has gone back to the roots of Neapolitan pizza: baked at 485°C in less than 60 seconds. Antipasti and home-made dolci and cake are also on offer.

● BRASSERIE MARIE
Zülpicher Strasse 268
(Sülz)
Tel. 0221/96269194
▲ Weyertal
◆ Tue-Sat from 6 pm
www.brasserie-marie.de

Paris feeling in Cologne. A cosy restaurant with outstanding french cuisine in relaxed atmosphere.

● HORNOCHSE
Neusser Strasse 304
(Nippes)
Tel. 0221/99758060
▲ Florastrasse
◆ Tue-Sun 12 noon-9pm
www.hornochse.koeln

A popular burger joint that also serves vegetarian and fish burgers.

● LA CANTINA DA PASQUALE
Marzellenstrasse 45–49
(city centre)
Tel. 0221/123778
▲ Dom/Hbf.
◆ Mon-Fri noon-3pm,
Mon-Sat 6pm-11pm
lacantinadapasquale.de

A small deli with a family atmosphere serving wonderful antipasti, delicious pasta and other Italian specialities, accompanied by selected wines.

● **FÄHRHAUS**
Steinstrasse 1
(Rodenkirchen)
Tel. 0221/9359969
▲ Heinrich-Lübke-Ufer
◆ from noon
www.faehrhauskoeln.de

The trip out to the historic ferry house in Rodenkirchen is worthwhile for its location on the Rhine and excellent Mediterranean dishes.

● **FISCHMARKT**
Am Bollwerk 21
(Old Town)
Tel. 0221/2576330
▲ Dom/Hbf.
◆ 10am-midnight
restaurantfischmarktkoeln.eatbu.com

A culinary attraction in the Old Town for those who enjoy something out of the ordinary, whether fish or meat dishes.

● **MAIBECK**
Am Frankenturm 5
(city centre)
Tel. 0221/96267300
▲ Dom/Hbf.
◆ Tue-Sun 12 noon-3pm, 6pm-midnight
www.maibeck.de

The highly successful concept here is top-quality cuisine without frills.

● **MAISON BLUE**
Im Ferkulum 18-22
(Südstadt)
▲ Chlodwigplatz
◆ Wed-Sat from 6pm
www.maisonblue-koeln.de

A wonderful little brasserie where you can enjoy delicious French specialities and game from the Eifel region.

● **NISH NUSH**
Aachener Straße 16
(Belgisches Viertel)
Tel. 0221/42335009
▲ Rudolfplatz
◆ Sun-Thu 11am-11.30pm, Fri-Sat 11-1am
www.facebook.com/NishNushCGN

Come here for Israeli streetfood – falafel, hummus, shawarma and lots of small plates for sharing!

● **SCAMPINO**
Deutz-Mülheimer Strasse 199 (Deutz)
Tel. 0221/618544
▲ Wiener Platz
◆ Mon-Fri noon-2pm, Mon-Sat 6pm-midnight, Sun 5pm-11pm
www.scampino.de

A rendezvous for lovers of Mediterranean fish dishes by the Mülheim harbour.

● **ZIPPIRI WEINBAR**
Aachener Strasse 259
(Braunsfeld)
Tel. 0221/42088451
▲ Melaten
◆ Do-Mo 6pm-11pm

The wine bar and restaurant Zippiri, which means rosemary in Sardinia, serves Italian meals with a Sardinian touch.

in Cologne – its towers reach a height of 157 metres. The tallest skyscraper is the Köln-Turm in the Mediapark at 148 metres, and the tallest on the right bank of the Rhine is the KölnTriangle (103 metres).

With 19 institutions of higher education and more than 100,000 students, Cologne is one of the three main university cities in Germany. For the media business Cologne is at the top, with five TV broadcasters and over 300 production companies. In the fields of art and culture, the city is also well provided for, with 40 museums and more than 100 galleries.

Cafés

COLOGNE CALENDAR

JANUARY
★ IMM Cologne
(furniture trade fair):
www.imm-cologne.de

FEBRUARY
★ Carnival:
www.koelnerkarneval.de

MARCH
★ Lit.Cologne
(literature festival):
www.litcologne.de

APRIL
★ c/o pop (Cologne Music
Festival): *c-o-pop.de*
★ Expedition Colonia
(city exploration festival):
expedition-colonia.de
★ International Women's
Film Festival Dortmund/
Cologne:
www.frauenfilmfestival.eu

MAY
★ Acht Brücken (festival
of modern music):
www.achtbruecken.de
★ Hännschen fair:
www.haenneschen.de

● **CAFÉ BAUTURM**
Aachener Strasse 24–26
(Belgisches Viertel)
▲ Rudolfplatz
◆ from 9am
www.cafe-bauturm.de

Breakfast all day – exis-
tentialist with a cup of
coffee and a cigarette,
or more luxurious with
Prosecco.

● **CAFÉ CENTRAL**
Jülicher Strasse 1
(Belgisches Viertel)
▲ Friesenplatz
◆ Mon-Fri 7am-11pm, Sat
8am-11pm, Sun 8am-10pm
www.cafecentralcologne.de

Outdoors beneath the
palms or in the black-
and-white artists' café,
you can spend the whole
day here, and sometimes
stay for live music in the
evening.

● **CAFÉ FRANCK**
Eichendorffstrasse 30
(Ehrenfeld)
▲ Subbelrather Strasse/
Gürtel
◆ Tue-Sun 10am-7pm,
Shibuya-Lounge:
Fri-Sat from 7pm (Sept-May)
www.cafe-franck.de/

A Cologne institution,
for delicious cream cakes

during the day and
creative cocktails in the
evening.

● **EISCAFE DOLCE
& GELATO**
Pfeilstrasse 51 (city centre)
▲ Rudolfplatz
◆ Mon-Sat 10am-11pm,
Sun 11am-11pm

Vanilla and chocolate
in traditional style, or
perhaps zuppa inglese
or pink grapefruit – this
family-run ice-cream par-
lour is one of the best in
Cologne.

● **FASSBENDER KÖLN**
Obenmarspforten 7
(Old Town)
▲ Heumarkt
◆ Mon-Sat 9.30am-
6.30pm, Sun 10am-6pm
www.fassbender.de

The circular room in 1950s style is an architectural attraction, and the charm of that era lives on here.

● **CAFÉ WALTER**
An der Bottmühle 13 (Südstadt)
▲ Chlodwigplatz
◆ Tue-Sun 10am-6pm
cafewalter.koeln

You can start the day with breakfast in a relaxing atmosphere and escape the hustle and bustle of the city.

● **LEUCHTE KAFFEEBAR**
Karolingerring 21 (Südstadt)
◆ Chlodwigplatz
◆ Mon-Fri 9am-6pm
Sat-Sun 10am-6pm

In this café on two levels, lovingly furnished in retro style, you can eat home-made cake and tasty quiches, all of it organic, fair-trade and regional.

● **CAFE KONDITOREI WAHLEN**
Hohenstaufenring 64 (city centre)
▲ Rudolfplatz
◆ Tue-Sun 11am-6pm
www.cafe-wahlen.de

Fancy a cream, fruit or buttercream cake? Or simply a dessert or biscuit? There's probably no better place in Cologne than this traditional confectioner's shop with its charming 1950s ambience.

● **SALON SCHMITZ**
Aachener Strasse 28 (Belgisches Viertel)
▲ Rudolfplatz
◆ From 9am
salonschmitz.com

For the first espresso of the day, quiche for lunch or a last drink in the evening, Salon Schmitz is always a good place to go.

● **THE COFFEE GANG**
Hohenstaufenring 19 (city centre)
▲ Zülpicher Platz
◆ Mon-Fri 8am-6pm,
Sat-Sun 10am-6pm
www.thecoffeegang.de

Coffee and espresso bar serving fair-trade products, freshly roasted. For the hungry there are New York cheesecakes and other homemade cakes or bread, pesto, tapenade and grilled vegetables.

● **TÖRTCHEN TÖRTCHEN**
Apostelnstrasse 19 (city centre)
▲ Rudolfplatz
◆ Mon-Sun 11am-8pm
www.toertchentoertchen.de

This pink and white shop and café is heaven if you love extravagant French patisserie.

COLOGNE CALENDAR

★ Photokina (leading global fair for imaging and video): *www.photokina.de*

JUNE
★ Summer entertainment: *www.sommer.koeln*

JULY
★ ColognePride (CSD street festival): *www.colognepride.de*
★ Summer festival: *www.bb-promotion.com/koelner-sommerfestival*
★ Summerjam (reggae festival): *summerjam.de*

AUGUST
★ Gamescom (leading fair for interactive games and entertainment): *www.gamescom.de*

OCTOBER
★ Köln Comedy Festival: *koelncomedy.de*
★ Generali Marathon: *koeln-marathon.de*

NOVEMBER
★ Art Cologne: *www.artcologne.de*
★ Short-film festival Köln: *kffk.de*

DECEMBER
★ Christmas markets: *www.koelntourismus.de*

SERVICE

Pubs, beer cellars & beer gardens

THE KÖLSCH MENU

Menus printed in dialect (Kölsch, the same as the word for the local beer) list regional specialities, mostly hearty dishes with names that need explanation even for German visitors to Cologne.

Ääppelschloot
Potato salad

Brodwoosch
Bratwurst, fried sausage

Hämmche
Pork knuckle, served with mashed potato and sauerkraut

Halve Hahn
A rye-bread roll with a slice of mature Dutch cheese, butter and mustard

Himmel un Äd
Fried Flönz (black pudding) with mashed potato and apple sauce

Kölsche Kaviar
Black pudding with onion rings

Rievkoche
Fried potato cakes like rösti

Soorbrode
Sour-marinated roast beef or horse meat

● ALCAZAR
Bismarckstrasse 39 a
(Belgisches Viertel)
Tel. 0221/515733
▲ Friesenplatz
◆ Mon-Sat noon-1am,
Sun 5pm-1am
www.alcazar-koeln.de

Thanks to its varied menu at reasonable prices and pleasant atmosphere, what was once a student pub has kept its popularity for decades.

● BOOTSHAUS ALBATROS
Rodenkirchener Leinpfad
(Rodenkirchen)
Tel. 0221/3508589
▲ Heinrich-Lübke-Ufer
◆ Tue-Sun noon-11pm
(April-Oct.) Tue-Fri 2pm-11pm, Sat-Sun noon-11pm
(Nov.-Mar.)
www.bootshaus-albatros.de

The "Bootshaus Albatros" is a houseboat with a beer garden and a great view of the Rhine and Rodenkirchen.

● BRÜSSELER
Brüsseler Platz 1
(Belgisches Viertel)
Tel. 0221/96028921
▲ Friedensplatz
◆ Tue-Thu 5pm-midnight,
Fri-Sat 2pm-3am
www.bruesseler-koeln.de

A pub on Brüsseler Platz for young and old. The interior blends industrial design with clerical items, outside you can watch the comings and goings on the square.

● FILOS
Merowingerstrasse 42
(Südstadt)
Tel. 0221/329147
▲ Chlodwigplatz
◆ 5pm-11pm
www.filoskoeln.de

A Südstadt institution, open for breakfast and late cocktails.

● GILDEN IM ZIMS
Heumarkt 77 (city centre)
Tel. 0221/16866110
▲ Heumarkt
◆ Mon-Fri from noon,
Sat-Sun from 11am
www.haus-zims.de

A hip Brauhaus pub in a historic building!

● HEISING & ADELMANN
Friesenstrasse 58-60
(Friesenviertel)
Tel. 0221/1309424
▲ Friesenplatz

◆ Thu-Sat from 6pm
*www.heising-und-
adelmann.de*

A trendy restaurant in
the Friesenviertel, where
guests often party until
the early hours.

● **KING GEORG**
Sudermanstraße 2
(Nordstadt)
Tel. 01806/570070
▲ Ebertplatz
◆ Mon-Thu 9pm-1am,
Fri-Sat 9pm-3.30am
www.kinggeorg.de

This small, high-class jazz
club with an ambitious
programme of live music
is a rendezvous for artists,
jazz lovers, night owls and
cocktail drinkers.

● **KM 689–COLOGNE
BEACH CLUB**
Rheinparkweg (Deutz)
Tel. 0221/2848610
▲ Bahnhof Deutz
◆ Tue-Thu from 2pm,
Fri-Sun from 1pm
(summer)
www.km689.de

On 3,500 square metres
of fine-grained sand you
can watch the sun go
down behind the Cologne
skyline or just chill out to
your heart's content.

● **LOMMERZHEIM**
Siegesstrasse 18 (Deutz)
Tel. 0221/814392
▲ Deutzer Freiheit
◆ Mon,Wed-Sun 11am-
2.30pm, 4.30pm-midnight
www.lommerzheim.koeln

A pub on the right bank
with cult status, antlers
on the walls and a creak-
ing wooden floor. The
thick, juicy pork chops are
legendary.

● **MAINZER HOF**
Mainzer Strasse/
Maternusstrasse 18
(Südstadt)
Tel. 0221/312549
▲ Ubierring
◆ from 5pm
www.mainzerhof-koeln.de

The "Südstadt living room"
serves delicious food and
is a good place to watch
the sun set.

● **PÄFFGEN BRAUHAUS**
Friesenstrasse 64–66
(Friesenviertel)
Tel. 0221/135461
▲ Friesenplatz
◆ Tue-Sun from noon
www.paeffgen-koelsch.de

The home of a brewery,
where the Päffgen family
have brewed with water
from their own well for
120 years. Don't expect it
to be modern and shiny
inside, but with its pleasant beer garden, heated
and covered in winter, this
is the city's most authentic Brauhaus (brewpub).

● **STADTGARTEN**
Venloer Strasse 40
(Belgisches Viertel)
Tel. 0221/9529940
▲ Friesenplatz
◆ Mon-Fri 4pm-midnight,
Sat 1pm-midnight
www.stadtgarten.de

One of Cologne's most
popular beer gardens at-
tracts a mixed crowd.

**BEWARE OF THE
WAITER!**

When drinking in a
Brauhaus, you need
to observe certain
rules! The waiter
here is called a
"Köbes" (from the
name Jakob), and
the tool of his trade
is a round tray from
which he places a

glass of Kölsch on
the table, unasked.
His uniform is a long
apron and a blue
knitted cardigan. He
is characterised by a
ready tongue, and it
is pointless to try to
argue with him.

SERVICE

Bars & Nightlife

Little Link

SUMMERJAM FESTIVAL

The first weekend in July is always festival time at Fühlinger See. Around 30,000 reggae fans from all over the world are drawn to the lake and its very special atmosphere for three days: a location on an island in the lake,

international and national top acts as well as young musicians and an audience from different generations, plus the possibility to camp around the lake. In its early days, the Summerjam Festival was purely a reggae festival with artists from the Caribbean and Africa, but over the years new influences from a wide variety of musical genres have been added. Today it stands for the best of reggae, dancehall and hiphop music.

www.summerjam.de

● BOOTSHAUS
Auenweg 173
(Mülheim)
▲ Deutz Messe/Deutz Bf
www.bootshaus.tv

One of the "best clubs in the world!"

● DIE KUNSTBAR
Chargesheimer Platz 1
(next to the central station, opposite the Alter Wartesaal/city centre)
▲ Dom/Hbf.
◆ Wed-Do from 8pm,
Fri-Sat from 9pm
www.diekunstbar.de

Here cocktails join an annually changing exhibition of works by an artist.

● LITTLE LINK
Maastrichter Strasse 20
(Belgisches Viertel)
▲ Friesenplatz
◆ Mon-Sat from 7pm
www.littlelink.de

A stylish bar and lounge with naked brick walls and innovative drinks.

● MONKEY BAR
(in 25hours Hotel The Circle)
Im Klapperhof 22-24
(Friesenviertel)
◆ Sun-Thu 5pm-1am,
Fri-Sat 5pm-2am
www.monkeybarkoeln.de

The rooftop bar is an ideal spot for communication and popular for its cocktail and long drink creations.

● ONA MOR
Roonstrasse 94
(Kwartier Latäng)
▲ Zülpicher Platz
◆ Wed-Sun from 8pm
www.onamor.de

A lovely cocktail bar with lots of its own recipes.

Lorbass
BAR & LOUNGE

● **SEIBERT'S**
Fliesenwall 33
(Friesenviertel)
▲ Friesenplatz
◆ Tue-Fri from 4pm,
Sun from 2pm
seiberts-bar.com

A classic bar in a historic
building with a wonder-
ful garden terrace in the
courtyard.

● **SIXPACK**
Aachener Strasse 33
(Belgisches Viertel)
▲ Rudolfplatz
◆ Wed-Sat from 8pm
sixpack-cologne.de

A legend in Cologne's
nightlife, serving many different sorts of bottled beer.

● **SPIRITS**
Engelbertstrasse 63
(Belgisches Viertel)
▲ Zülpicher Platz
◆ Mon-Thu 6pm-1am,
Fri-Sat 6pm-3am
www.spiritsbar.de

A trendy joint in the
Belgisches Viertel, where
the surroundings, drinks,
service and sound are all
just right.

● **THE GRID BAR**
Friesenstrasse 62
(Friesenviertel)
▲ Friesenplatz
◆ Tue-Sat from 7pm,
Sun from 5pm
www.thegridbar.de

Hidden away behind a
small door (please ring
the bell!!), the world-class
bartender Marian Krause
mixes high-quality drinks.
The covered terrace is
home to Cologne's first
Outdoor Davidoff Cigar
Lounge.

● **TSUNAMI**
Im Ferkulum 9
(Severinsviertel)
▲ Chlodwigplatz
◆ Fri-Sat from 11pm
www.tsunami-club.de

Music club with indie,
punk rock, rock 'n' roll and
more, but not mainstream.

WOHNGEMEINSCHAFT
Richard-Wagner-Strasse 39
(Belgisches Viertel)
▲ Rudolfplatz
◆ Sun-Thu 3pm-2am,
Fri-Sat 3pm-3am
*www.die-wohngemein
schaft.net/cafebar*

Cake in the afternoon,
a bar in the evenings,
sometimes with a DJ,
sometimes without: this
café-bar is a place where
people passing through
and long-established Co-
logne residents meet. Outdoor terrace in summer!

C/O POP FESTIVAL

In June international
stars, celebrated newcom-
ers and up-and-coming
unknowns come to
Cologne's music venues
when the c/o pop festival
gets going. For five days,
more than 80 bands, art-
ists and DJs can be heard
in over 30 different con-
cert halls, clubs, bars and
open-air venues, both in
the city centre and further
out. For more than ten

years this music festival
for electronic pop music
has been an established
feature of the event cal-
endar. At the same time
a specialist event for the
latest issues in the business, the c/o pop Conven-
tion, and SoundTrack_Co-
logne, the biggest German
congress for music and
sound in film, games and
media, take place.

c-o-pop.de
www.soundtrackcologne.de

Culture

GÜRZENICH ORCHESTRA

Robert and Clara Schumann played with this orchestra, Giuseppe Verdi and Richard Wagner conducted their latest works with it, Richard Strauss chose it for the world premiere of *Till Eulenspiegel* (1895) and *Don Quixote* (1898), Gustav Mahler for his 5th symphony. The list of principal conductors ranges from Conradin Kreutzer and Hermann Abendroth to Markus Stenz and, at present, François-Xavier Roth. Named after the festival hall in which it performed for decades, today the Gürzenich-Orchester is one Germany's

longest-established symphony orchestras. Its base is the Philharmonie in Cologne, and it plays for the Cologne opera. Its project "GO live!", in which performances in the Philharmonie are recorded live and can be purchased immediately after the concert, is unique worldwide.

www.guerzenich-orchester.de

THEATRE

● ARTHEATER
Ehrenfeldgürtel 127
(Ehrenfeld)
Tel. 0221/5509960
▲ Subbelrather Strasse/
Gürtel
artheater.info/11/

A young theatre that aims to stage dramatic work of different cultures and styles under one roof.

● ATELIER THEATER
Roonstrasse 78
(Kwartier Latäng)
Tel. 0221/242485
▲ Zülpicher Platz
ateliertheater.de

A small basement theatre with an innovative cabaret programme directed by the satirist Rosa K. Wirtz.

● BÜHNE DER KULTUREN
Platenstrasse 32
(Ehrenfeld)
Tel. 0221/9559510
▲ Subbelrather Strasse/
Gürtel
www.buehnederkulturen.de

Members of the ensemble are of various nationalities and religions, and wish to convey this cultural diversity by artistic means.

● COMEDIA COLONIA
Vondelstrasse 4–8
(Südstadt)
Tel. 0221/88877222
▲ Chlodwigplatz,
Ulrepforte
www.comedia-koeln.de/

With a love of experimentation and a programme of cabaret and satire that has a national reputation, the Comedia is well-known beyond the city of Cologne.

● FREIES WERKSTATT-THEATER
Zugweg 10 (Südstadt)
Tel. 0221/327817
▲ Chlodwigplatz
www.fwt-koeln.de

Known for 20 years for its work in experimental theatre.

● HÄNNESCHEN-THEATER
Eisenmarkt 2–4 (Old Town)
Tel. 0221/2581201
▲ Heumarkt
www.haenneschen.de

The puppets speaking Cologne dialect have been a local institution for 200 years – unfortunately almost always sold out.

● **HORIZONT THEATER**
Thürmchenswall 25
(Nordstadt)
Tel. 0221/131604
▲ Ebertplatz
www.horizont-theater.de

One of the city's best-known and most renowned independent theatres, with a programme characterised by humour and delight in acting, on a basement stage at the heart of the city.

● **KLÜNGELPÜTZ**
Gertrudenstrasse 24
(city centre)
Tel. 0152/04443368
▲ Neumarkt
kluengelpuetz.de

Sharp and witty political satire.

● **SCHAUSPIELHAUS**
Schanzenstrasse 6–20
(Mülheim)
Tel. 0221/22128400
▲ Keupstrasse
www.schauspiel.koeln

The municipal theatre company directed by Stefan Bachmann plays on the Carlswerk site. Its programme ranges from classic and contemporary dramas to theatrical treatments of current issues in society.

● **SENFTÖPFCHEN**
Grosse Neugasse 2–4
(Old Town)
Tel. 0221/2581058
▲ Dom/Hbf.
www.senftoepfrhen-theater.dc

For over 40 years a popular venue for cabaret, chansons and other small-scale performances, where relatively unknown performers are given the chance to shine.

● **STUDIOBÜHNE KÖLN**
Universitätsstrasse 16 a
(Sülz)
Tel. 0221/4704513
▲ Universität
studiobuehnekoeln.de

Germany's oldest university theatre is known for its experimental style and visits by touring companies.

● **THEATER AM DOM**
Glockengasse 11
(city centre)
Tel. 0221/2580153
▲ Neumarkt
www.theateramdom.de

Comedy and farce, with guest appearances by well-known actors.

● **THEATER DER KELLER IN TANZFAKTUR**
Siegburger Strasse 233W
(Deutz)
Tel. 0221/318059
▲ Poller Kirchweg
www.theater-der-keller.de

The oldest independent theatre in Cologne devotes itself to contemporary works.

INTERNATIONAL COMEDY FESTIVAL

For stand-up comedy and variety performances, for musical and literary cabaret, for the last 25 years the biggest comedy festival in Germany has been held in Cologne in October. More than 150 artists, both stars and unknown newcomers, present a diverse programme of outstandingly good entertainment in more than 100 shows at some 20 venues over a two-week period. The festival kicks off with its legendary opening show "Cologne lacht!" (laughs). One of the highlights is the 1Live Köln Comedy-Nacht XXL – Europe's biggest comedy show. During the festival the Deutscher Comedy-Preis is awarded in various categories in the Coloneum, an event that is later broadcast live on the RTL the TV channel.

www.comedy.cologne

SERVICE

Culture

LIT.COLOGNE

The absolute highlight of the year in the city's literature scene is Lit.Cologne, which has taken place each year since 2001. It is Europe's biggest literary festival, attracting large audiences, including well-attended readings and discussions in English with major English-speaking authors. Lasting eleven days, it con-

sists of more than 175 events at a variety of venues, with over 200 authors and artists. The programme is a high-calibre mix of international and German-language literature, from bestsellers to newcomers. A feature is the encounter of authors with artists from different disciplines. Lit.Kid is a series of cultural events for children with almost 90 performances.

www.litcologne.de

● **THEATER IM BAUTURM**
Aachener Strasse 24
(Belgisches Viertel)
Tel. 0221/524242
▲ Rudolfplatz
www.theaterimbauturm.de

A contemporary theatre with literary ambitions that stages a diverse, high-quality programme with its own productions.

● **THEATER TIEFROT**
Dagobertstrasse 32
(Nordstadt)
Tel. 0221/4600911
▲ Ebertplatz
www.theater-tiefrot.com

A small private theatre run by the actor and director Volker Lippmann in the cellar vault of the Hopper Hotel St. Antonius.

● **VOLKSBÜHNE AM RUDOLFPLATZ**
Aachener Strasse 5
(Belgisches Viertel)
Tel. 0221/251747
▲ Rudolfplatz
www.volksbuehne-rudolfplatz.de

The famous Volkstheater Millowitsch plays in Cologne's oldest theatre. At other times the stage is free for music, political satire, comedy and cabaret.

MUSIC

● **ALTES PFANDHAUS**
Kartäuserwall 20
(Südstadt)
Tel. 0221/2783685
▲ Chlodwigplatz
www.altes-pfandhaus.de

● **HOCHSCHULE FÜR MUSIK UND TANZ**
Unter Krahnenbäumen 87
(Nordstadt)
Tel. 0221/9128180
▲ Ebertplatz
www.hfmt-koeln.de

Frequently the students put on high-quality performances of classical music and jazz.

● **LOFT**
Wissmannstrasse 30
(Ehrenfeld)
Tel. 0221/9521555
▲ Körnerstrasse
www.loftkoeln.de

A venue for improvised music, contemporary music and jazz on one floor of a converted factory.

● **MUSICAL DOME**
Goldgasse 1/Breslauer Platz (city centre)
Tel. 0180/6806555
▲ Breslauer Platz
www.musicaldome.de

In the big blue tent behind the central station, productions of various musicals are staged.

● **OPER DER STADT KÖLN**
Rheinparkweg 1 (Deutz)
Tel. 0221/22128400
▲ Bahnhof Deutz
www.oper.koeln

The city opera ensemble is currently performing in the Staatenhaus on the right bank while the opera house is renovated.

● **PHILHARMONIE**
Bischofsgartenstrasse 1 (city centre)
Tel. 0221/280280
▲ Dom/Hbf.
www.koelner-philharmonie.de

Modelled on an amphitheatre, this concert hall is known for its outstanding architecture and excellent acoustics, as well as for the quality of its programme.

CINEMAS

● **CINEDOM**
Im Mediapark 1 (Nordstadt)
Tel. 0221/95195107
▲ Christophstrasse/Mediapark
www.cinedom.de

A big, modern multiplex cinema with the latest projection and sound technology, where all the latest mainstream movies are screened.

● **FILMPALETTE**
Lübecker Strasse 15 (Nordstadt)
Tel. 0221/122112
▲ Ebertplatz
www.filmpalette-koeln.de

This 80-seater screens low-budget productions, and is a forum for trash films and art films.

● **METROPOLIS**
Ebertplatz 19 (Nordstadt)
Tel. 0221/7391245
▲ Ebertplatz
metropolis-koeln.de

English-language films can be seen here in the original version. It is also a venue for premieres and good children's cinema.

LITERATURE

● **LITERATURHAUS KÖLN E. V.**
Grosser Griechenmarkt 39 (city centre)
Tel. 0221/9955580
▲ Poststrasse
literaturhaus-koeln.de

Debutants and holders of the Nobel Prize for Literature, authors and readers of children's books and contemporary literature meet here for varied activities.

MEDIAPARK

One of Cologne's most prominent urban development projects of the 1990s is the Mediapark on the site of old railway freight yards. Embedded in a park landscape with a lake are companies and educational institutions from the fields of media, IT, culture, education, medicine, research and trade, as well as a hotel, shops, restaurants, the city's first multiplex cinema and housing. Planned by the Canadian architect Eberhard Zedier, and radiating from a central open space, is an architectural ensemble of seven-storey buildings and the 148-metre-high KölnTurm with a façade by Jean Nouvel that reflects the panorama of Cologne.

www.mediapark.de

SERVICE

Museums

MUSEUM SCHNÜTGEN

What more effective place could there be to present Christian art than the interior of a Romanesque basilica? St Cäcilien, once a collegiate church, is a unique setting for masterpieces from more than 800 years that provide insights into the life and thought of the Middle Ages and tell fascinating stories. In the church and a new exhibition space in the Kulturquartier on Neumarkt, visitors can learn about the radiance and the message of stained glass windows, about how art was converted to gold with the famous Golden Panel from St Ursula as an example, or about the medieval trade in paper-maché copies and clay-pipe miniatures of well-known saints' images.

Cäcilienstrasse 29–33
(city centre)
Tel. 0221/22131355
▲ *Poststrasse*
◆ *Tue-Sun 10am-6pm,*
Thu until 8pm
www.museum-schnuetgen.de

● **DUFTMUSEUM (PERFUME)**
➤ p. 16

● **EL-DE-HAUS**
(NS-Documentation Center)
Appellhofplatz 23–25
(city centre)
Tel. 0221/22126331
▲ Appellhofplatz
◆ Tue-Fri 10am-6pm, Sat-Sun 11am-6pm, first Thu in the month 10am-10pm
www.museenkoeln.de/ns-dokumentationszentrum

Exhibition on Cologne under National Socialism.

● **KÄTHE-KOLLWITZ-MUSEUM**
Neumarkt 18–24
(city centre)
Tel. 0221/2272899
▲ Neumarkt
◆ Tue-Sun 11am-6pm, guided tours Sun 3pm, Thu 5pm
www.kollwitz.de

The world's biggest collection of the art of Käthe Kollwitz.

● **KÖLNER KARNEVALS-MUSEUM**
Maarweg 134–136
(Braunsfeld)
Tel. 0221/5740031
(guided tours)
▲ Maarweg
◆ Currently closed
www.koelnerkarnevals museum.de

The museum examines Carnival as a cultural phenomenon and its practices.

● **KÖLNISCHES STADTMUSEUM**
Minoritenstrasse 13
(city centre)
Tel. 0221/22122398
▲ Dom/Hbf.
◆ opening end of 2023
www.museenkoeln.de/ksm

The history, intellectual, economic and everyday life of Cologne.

● **KOLUMBA** ➤ p. 32

● **KUNSTSTATION ST. PETER**
Leonhard-Tietz-Strasse 6
(city centre)
Tel. 0221/9213030
▲ Neumarkt
◆ Tue-Fri 10am-noon
www.sankt-peter-koeln.de

A dialogue between a church and art, between art and religion.

● **KUNSTVEREIN**
Hahnenstrasse 6
(city centre)
Tel. 0221/217021
▲ Rudolfplatz
◆ Tue-Sun 11am-6pm
koelnischerkunstverein.de

The purpose of the association is to promote contemporary art.

● MUSEUM DES DEUTSCHEN TANZ-ARCHIVS KÖLN
Im Mediapark 7 (3rd floor) (Nordstadt)
Tel. 0221/88595400
▲ Christophstrasse/ Mediapark
◆ Thu-Mon 2am-7pm
www.deutsches-tanzarchiv. de/museum

Exhibition about the history of dance.

● MUSEUM FÜR ANGEWANDTE KUNST
An der Rechtschule (city centre)
Tel. 0221/22126714
▲ Dom/Hbf.
◆ Tue-Sun 10am-6pm, first Thu in the month 10am-10pm
museenkoeln.de/portal/ MAKK

European arts and crafts from the Middle Ages to the present.

● MUSEUM LUDWIG
➤ p. 46

● MUSEUM FÜR OSTASIATISCHE KUNST
Universitätsstrasse 100 (Lindenthal)
Tel. 0221/22128608
▲ Universitätsstrasse
◆ Tue-Sun 11am-5pm, first Thu in the month 11am-10pm
www.museen koeln.de/mok

Collections of Chinese, Japanese and Korean art.

● ODYSSEUM
Corintostrasse 1 (Kalk)
Tel. 0221/69068111
▲ Kalk Post, Trimbornstrasse
◆ Fri 2am-7pm, Sat-Sun 10am-7pm
www.odysseum.de

An interactive science adventure park for the whole family.

● RAUTENSTRAUCH-JOEST-MUSEUM
Cäcilienstrasse 29–33 (city centre)
Tel. 0221/22131356
▲ Neumarkt
◆ Tue-Wed, Fri-Sun 10am-6pm, Thu 10am-8pm
www.museenkoeln.de/rautenstrauch-joest-museum/ Besuch

Exhibitions about life in non-European cultures.

● RÖMISCH-GERMA-NISCHES MUSEUM
Cäcilienstrasse 46 (city centre)
Tel. 0221/22128094 und 22128095
▲ Neumarkt
◆ Wed-Mon 10am-6pm
www.roemisch-germanisches-museum.de

Daily life in Roman Cologne.

● SCHOKOLADEN-MUSEUM
➤ p. 40

● SPORT- UND OLYMPIAMUSEUM
➤ p. 41

● WALLRAF-RICHARTZ-MUSEUM
➤ p. 47

SCULPTURE PARK

The Skulpturenpark close to the zoo is a special place to take a walk. The exhibition entitled *KölnSkulptur* with its changing works presents trends in contemporary sculpture, seeing this art as an idea that relates to the existing situation. It is a place that gives

Sculpture by Amalia Ulman

visitors time – time to linger, moments to contemplate a range of different materials. The present exhibition of contemporary works, the eighth so far, goes back to a private initiative by the collectors Michael and Eleonore Stoffel.

Main entrance: Riehler Strasse (near Zoobrücke)
▲ *Zoo/Flora*
◆ *10.30am-7pm (April-Sept) 10.30am-5pm (Oct-March)*
www.skulpturen parkkoeln.de

Shopping

EAU DE COLOGNE

Not many people know that eau de Cologne used to be a panacea for all ills. Inhaled, drunk or worn on the skin, it was thought to be a protection against plague. An "aqua admirabile" (miracle water) was produced in Cologne as long ago as the late 17th century, but it was not until French army officers used it to counteract the bad smells in the city during the Seven Years' War (1756–63) that a medicinal product came to be used as a perfume under a name now known worldwide: eau de Cologne.

● **4711-HAUS**
Glockengasse 4
(city centre)
▲ Appellhofplatz
◆ Mon-Fri 9.30am-6.30pm, Sat 9.30am-6pm
www.4711.com

Here you can buy all the perfume products of the 4711 brand and also sample this famous eau de Cologne from a fountain.

● **ADIEU TRISTESSE**
Moltkestrasse 85
(Belgisches Viertel)
▲ Moltkestrasse
◆ Tue-Thu 10am-1pm, 2-6pm, Sat noon-4pm
www.facebook.com/Adieu-Tristesse

Soft toys, cushions and children's clothing – everything on sale here is a one-off, yet these unique products, made with love, are affordable.

● **BÄRENDRECK APOTHEKE**
Richard-Wagner-Strasse 1
(city centre)
▲ Rudolfplatz
◆ Tue-Fri 12 noon-6.30pm, Sat 12 noon-4.30pm
www.baerendreck-apotheke.de

Everything to do with liquorice, from liquorice mustard to liquorice soap and toothpaste, and more than 600 kinds of liquorice to eat.

● **BUCHHANDLUNG WALTER KÖNIG**
Ehrenstrasse 4
(city centre)
▲ Friesenplatz
◆ Mo-Sat 10am-6pm
www.buchhandlung-walther-koenig.de

You can recognise this exquisite bookshop by the "tumbling books" on its corner building. A veritable paradise for bibliophiles, who can find books about art, architecture, photography, cinema, fashion and design.

● **DIE TAGEDIEBE**
Hirschgässchen 1
(Südstadt)
▲ Ubierring
◆ Mon-Fri 11am-7pm, Sat 11am-6pm
www.die-tagediebe.com

Books and many other beautiful things.

● **DIE WERKSTATT**
An der Eiche 9
(Südstadt)
▲ Chlodwigplatz
◆ Mon-Fri 12 noon-7pm,
Sat 11am-3pm
www.die-werkstatt-koeln.de

Porcelain jewellery and
home accessories are
made here.

● **DOMSHOP**
Roncalliplatz
(city centre)
▲ Dom/Hbf.
◆ Mon-Sat 10am-7pm
Sun 11am-7pm seasonal
*www.koelner-dom.de/
besuchen/domshop*

For a cast of a gargoyle,
a cookie-cutter, biscuits
in the shape of the
cathedral tower or a
rosary – buy here to
support the cathedral.

● **HERNANDO CORTEZ
SCHOKOLADEN**
Gertrudenstrasse 23
(city centre)
▲ Friesenplatz
◆ Mon-Sat 10am-7pm
www.hernando-cortez.de

Here you can order a cup
of drinking chocolate and
buy the finest chocolate
from all around the world.

● **HONIG MÜNGERSDORFF**
An St. Agatha 37
(city centre)
▲ Heumarkt
◆ Mon-Fri 9am-1pm,
2pm-5pm, Sat 9am-noon
(Sept.-April)
www.honig-muengersdorff.de

For over 150 years this
specialist shop has sold
everything connected
with honey, from mead to
honey sweets and liqueur.

● **KÖLNSHOP**
(in Kölntourismus)
Kardinal-Höffner-Platz 1
(city centre)
▲ Dom/Hbf.
◆ Mon-Tue, Thu-Sat
9am-7pm
www.der-koelnshop.de

For fruit gums in the
shape of the cathedral or
a Cologne egg-timer, for
local souvenires the shop
in the tourist office is a
good source!

● **LOFT 43**
Marzellenstrasse 43
(city centre)
▲ Dom/Hbf.
◆ Tue-Fri 12 noon-8pm,
Sat 2-8pm
www.loft43.eu

Vintage furniture covering
decades of design from
the 1920s to the 1980s.

● **MAUS&MEHR**
Breite Strasse 6–26/
WDR-Arkaden (city centre)
▲ Appellhofplatz
◆ Mon-Sat 10am-6.30pm
mausundmehr.com

This is the merchandis-
ing outlet for all kinds of
products associated with
popular characters from
the programmes of the
broadcaster WDR, includ-
ing the Mouse and Captain
Bluebear.

TRADE FAIRS

On the right bank of
the Rhine, behind the
80-metre-tall tower (Mes-
seturm) and the historic
trade-fair halls now oc-
cupied by the RTL broad-
caster, lie the grounds of
Kölnmesse, the world's
fourth-biggest trade-fair
site, with 11 exhibition
halls covering 284,000
square metres and
100,000 square metres of
open space. Around three
million visitors from over
200 countries and some
54,000 exhibitors from
more than 120 countries
come here every year
to take part in over 80
specialist trade shows in
more 25 business sectors,
including leading global
fairs.

www.koelnmesse.de

Useful Addresses

"WE'RE GOING TO FC KÖLLE ..."

... means a trip to the stadium of 1. FC Köln – Cologne Football Club, founded in 1948. It may not be as old as some other German clubs, but has a great tradition. Hennes Weisweiler, Wolfgang Overath and Bernd Schuster are just a few of the famous players who have trodden the turf here. 1. FC Köln won the first-ever Bundesliga champion-

ship and put its stamp on German professional football for many years. The most remarkable thing about the club are its fans. It is not easy to get hold of a season ticket, and even when the team is not performing well, the loyalty of the fans in the Rhein-energie-Stadion is not shaken. At every home game they sing their favourite anthem, with the words "We're true to you, FC Kölle".

www.fc.de

INFORMATION

KÖLNTOURISMUS GMBH
Kardinal-Höffner-Platz 1
50667 Köln
Tel. 0221/346430
◆ Mon-Tue, Thu-Sat
9am-7pm,
www.koelntourismus.de

ARRIVAL/DEPARTURE

● BY AIR: Cologne-Bonn Airport lies east of Cologne, about 17 kilometres from the city centre.
Tel. 02203/404001
For the latest information about departures and arrivals, see the website
www.koeln-bonn-airport.de

LOCAL TRAINS (S-BAHN): lines 13 (destination Köln-Ehrenfeld) and 19 (destination Horrem) and regional trains RE 8 and RE 6 go to Cologne's central station in approx. 15 minutes. For further connections to intercity, regional express and local trains, refer to
www.koeln-bonn-airport.de/ parken-anreise/bus-bahn.html

TAXI: taxi ranks are next to the exits on the arrivals level. To get an idea of the costs, see
www.koeln-bonn-airport.de/ parken-anreise/taxi.html

CAR HIRE offices are in terminal 2 on level 0:
www.koeln-bonn-airport.de/ parken-anreise/mietwagen.html
By car it takes around 25 minutes to reach the city centre via autobahn A 59.

● OVERLAND BUS: a cheap way of reaching Cologne from other German cities and abroad is to take a long-distance bus. The new bus station is at the airport.

● RAIL: there are convenient rail connections from many European countries, with more than 1,300 trains from abroad and other German cities arriving daily in Cologne. Service hotline
Tel. 030/2970
www.bahn.de

Connections to the central station (Hauptbahnhof; *www.bahnhof.de/koeln-hbf*): local trains S 6, S 11, S 12 and S 13, trams 5,16 and 18 to the subway stations Dom/Hbf and Breslauer Platz, buses 132, 133, 250, 260 and 978 to Dom/Hbf.

TAXIS are on the right when leaving the station on the cathedral side; on the other side they stop at the north end of Breslauer Platz.

BICYCLES: there is a bike-hire station on Breslauer Platz, exit A, about 50 metres towards the river Rhine.
www.callabike-interaktiv.de

HIRE CARS: various companies, see rail information for Flinkster and in the passage opposite the travel centre Sixt, Europcar, Avis.

● CAR: Cologne is surrounded by an orbital highway from which ten highways radiate in all directions (A 1, A 3, A 4, A 57, A 59, A 555, A 559). For park and ride, see *www.kvb.koeln/fahrtinfo/ park_and_ride.html* Note that only vehicles with a green environmental sign for emissions class 4 may enter Cologne city centre.

BANKS

◆ All major German banks have branches in Cologne city centre (on Unter Sachsenhausen, Neumarkt, Hohenzollern- and Habsburgerring), open at the usual times, generally 8.30am-4pm.

ReiseBank Köln
· Hauptbahnhof
Tel. 0221/134403
◆ Mon-Fri 8am-7pm, Sat 8am-6pm, Sun 8am-5pm

TICKET SALES

KölnTicket
Bischofsgartenstrasse 1
Tel. 0221/2801
www.koelnticket.de

Theaterkasse Neumarkt
in the subway passage on Neumarkt
Tel. 0221/42076000

EMERGENCY

Police Tel. 110
Fire dept. Tel. 112
Emergency doctor
Tel. 116117
Emergency dentist
Tel. 01805/986700
Emergency pharmacy:
www.aponet.de
Lost and found:
www.stadt-koeln.de/service/ adressen/fundbuero

PUBLIC TRANSPORT

Kölner Verkehrsbetriebe (KVB)
www.kvb-koeln.de
Timetables and fares
Tel. 01806/504030
Tickets: customer centre on Neumarkt (subway)
◆ Mon-Fri 8am-8pm, Sat 8.30am-6pm

POST

Main post office in WDR-Arkaden
Breite Strasse 6–26
◆ Mon-Fri 8am-6pm, Sat 9am-2pm

CITY TOURS

KölnTourismus (tourist office)
Tel. 0221/346430
www.koelntourismus.de/ buchen-kaufen/ stadtfuehrungen

Domforum (cathedral)
Roncalliplatz 2
Tel. 0221/92584730
www.domforum.de
◆ Mon-Fri 10am-noon, Mo-Thu 1pm-3pm

Inside Cologne
Bismarckstrasse 70
Tel. 0221/521977
www.insidecologne.de

Kölner Frauen-geschichtsverein (women's history)
Marienplatz 4
Tel. 0221/79002929
www.frauengeschichts verein.de

RegioColonia e.V.
Marienplatz 4
Tel. 0221/9654595
www.regiocolonia.de

Segway Tour Köln
Tel. 0221/27260597
www.seg-tour-koeln.de

StattReisen Köln
Bürgerstrasse 4
Tel. 0221/7325113
www.stattreisen-koeln.de

Verein Kölner Stadtführer e.V.
Tel. 01520/5119673
www.koelner-stadtfuehrer.de

TAXI

Tel. 0221/2882
or 19410

3⁺ TIP The KölnCard gives you free trips on local public transport for either 24 or 48 hours and up to 50 per cent discount for services in the fields of art, culture and eating out. The KölnCard is on sale at the KölnTourismus Service Centre opposite the cathedral and from all ticket machines of the KVB and DB (rail operator), in many hotels/hostels and from a number of travel agents.
www.cologne-tourism. com/book-buy/koelncard/

Cologne's History

38 BC The Roman general Agrippa brings the Germanic Ubii tribe to the left bank of the Rhine and founds the Oppidum Ubiorum.

50 BC Emperor Claudius, at the prompting of his wife Agrippina, raises the status of the town, giving it the name Colonia Claudia Ara Agrippinensium, CCAA for short.

90 CCAA becomes capital of Lower Germany; the governor resides in the Praetorium.

c. 310 Emperor Constantine builds the military camp Divitia (Deutz today) on the right bank of the Rhine to secure the border and links it to the Roman town with a bridge.

c. 313 Maternus is the first named bishop of Cologne.

454 The Franks become rulers of the city.

c. 790 Charlemagne makes Cologne an archdiocese, headed by Archbishop Hildebold.

953 Emperor Otto I gives his brother, Archbishop Bruno of Cologne, the Duchy of Lorraine – putting religious and secular power in the same hands for the first time.

1164 Archbishop Rainald von Dassel brings the bones of the Three Magi to Cologne.

from 1180 Through the third extension of its boundaries, Cologne becomes the biggest city in the empire.

1248 Archbishop Konrad von Hochstaden lays the foundation stone of the new cathedral.

1288 Cologne's citizens get their political independence from the archbishop in the Battle of Worringen.

1388 The first municipal university in Germany is established in Cologne.

1396 The guilds of artisans issue a democratic constitution of the city and take power from the patrician families.